1ˢᵗ World Library Literary Society

Giving Back to the World

"If you want to work on the core problem, it's early school literacy."

- James Barksdale, former CEO of Netscape

"No skill is more crucial to the future of a child, or to a democratic and prosperous society, than literacy."

- Los Angeles Times

"Literacy... means far more than learning how to read and write... The aim is to transmit... knowledge and promote social participation."

- UNESCO

"Literacy is not a luxury, it is a right and a responsibility. If our world is to meet the challenges of the twenty-first century we must harness the energy and creativity of all our citizens."

- President Bill Clinton

"Parents should be encouraged to read to their children, and teachers should be equipped with all available techniques for teaching literacy, so the varying needs and capacities of individual kids can be taken into account."

- Hugh Mackay

THE GILPINS

AND THEIR FORTUNES

A STORY OF EARLY DAYS IN AUSTRALIA

W. H. G. KINGSTON

1st WORLD LIBRARY Literary Society

The Gilpins and their Fortunes

William H. G. Kingston

© 1st World Library, 2007
PO Box 2211
Fairfield, IA 52556
www.1stworldlibrary.com
First Edition

LCCN: 2007934219

Softcover ISBN: 978-1-4218-9685-4
Hardcover ISBN: 978-1-4218-9785-1
eBook ISBN: 978-1-4218-9585-7

Purchase *"The Gilpins and their Fortunes"*
as a traditional bound book at:
www.1stWorldLibrary.com/purchase.asp?ISBN=978-1-4218-9685-4

1st World Library is a literary, educational organization
dedicated to:

- Creating a free internet library of downloadable ebooks

- Hosting writing competitions and offering book publishing
scholarships.

Interested in more 1st World Library books? contact:
literacy@1stworldlibrary.com
Check us out at: www.1stworldlibrary.com

CHAPTER ONE

Arthur Gilpin and Mark Withers walked down the High Street, arm-in-arm, on their return to their respective homes from the well-managed school of Wallington.

They were among the head boys, and were on the point of leaving it to enter on the work of active life, and make their way in the world. They had often of late discussed the important question—all-important, as it seemed to them— "How are we to make our way—to gain wealth, influence, our hearts' desires?"

"For my part, I cannot stand a plodding style of doing things," said Mark. "It is all very well for those without brains, but a fellow who has a grain of sense in his head requires a more rapid way of making a fortune. Life is too short to be wasted in getting money. I want to have it to spend while I am young and can enjoy it."

Arthur was silent for some time. At length he remarked, "It strikes me, Mark, that the object of making money is that we may support ourselves and families, and help those who are in distress. My father often says to James, and to me, and to the rest of us, 'I don't want you, when you enter business, to be thinking only how you can make money. Do your duty, and act liberally towards all men, and you will have a sufficiency at all events, if not wealth.'"

"Oh! your father's old-fashioned notions won't do in the world, and certainly won't suit me, that I can tell you," answered Mark, in a scornful tone.

"My father is considered a sensible man. What he preaches he practises; and though he has a very large family, no one calls him a poor man," argued Arthur. "He says that, considering how short life is, it cannot be wise to spend the time, as many men do, in gathering up riches and setting so high a value on them. But here comes James! Let us hear what he has to say on the subject."

"Oh! of course, James has got the same notions from your father that you have, and I am not going to be influenced by him," answered Withers.

James, however, was appealed to, and answered, "Even if we were to live for ever in this world, I should agree with Arthur; for, from all I see and hear, I am convinced that wealth cannot secure happiness; but as this world is only a place of preparation for another, it is evident folly to set one's heart upon what must be so soon parted with."

Withers made a gesture of impatience, exclaiming, "Come, come, I won't stand any preaching, you know that; but we are old friends, and so I don't want to quarrel about trifles, when we are so soon to separate! You stick to your opinion, I will stick to mine, and we'll see who is right at last."

"If this matter were a trifle I would not press it, but, because I am sure that it is one of great importance, I do press it upon you most earnestly, though, believe me, I am sorry to annoy you," said Arthur Gilpin.

W. H. G. Kingston

"Oh! I dare say you mean well," answered Withers, in a contemptuous tone. "But don't bother me again on the subject, there's a good fellow. You, James, are so above me, that I don't pretend to understand what you mean." Saying this with a condescending air, he shook hands with the two brothers, and entered the house of his father, who was the principal solicitor of the town.

The two Gilpins walked on towards their home. Their father possessed a small landed property, which he farmed himself. He had a very numerous family, and though hitherto he had been able to keep them together with advantage, the time had arrived when some of them must go forth to provide for themselves in the world. James and Arthur had long turned their thoughts towards Australia, for which part of the British possessions they were preparing to take their departure. Mr Gilpin, or the squire, as he was called, was looked upon as an upright, kind-hearted man. He was sensible, well educated, and a true Christian; and he brought up his children in the fear and admonition of the Lord.

A year passed by: a long sea voyage was over, and James and Arthur Gilpin stood on the shores of Australia. Two other brothers, with their sisters, remained to help their father in his farm at home. James and Arthur had left England, stout of heart, and resolved to do their duty, hoping to establish a comfortable home for themselves and for those who might come after them. Their ship lay close to the broad quay of the magnificent capital of New South Wales. They had scarcely been prepared for the scene of beauty and grandeur which met their sight as they entered Port Jackson, the harbour of Sydney, with its lofty and picturesque shores, every available spot occupied by some ornamental villa or building of greater pretension, numerous romantic inlets and indentations running up towards the north; while the city itself appeared extending far away inland with its broad, well-built streets, its numberless churches, colleges, public schools, hospitals, banks, government buildings, and other public and private edifices, too numerous to be mentioned.

The Gilpins, as they were put on shore with their luggage, felt themselves almost lost in that great city. They were dressed in their rough, every-day suits, and looked simple, hardworking country lads, and younger than they really were.

Large as Sydney then was, it was still diminutive compared to what it has since become. Founded by criminals, it was unhappily as far advanced in crime and wickedness as the oldest cities of the old world, though efforts were being then made, as they have ever since continued to be made, and, happily, not without some degree of success, to wipe out the stain. The two brothers stood for some time watching the bustling scene before them. Huge drays laden with bales of wool were slowly moving along the quay towards the ships taking in cargo, while porters, and carts, with ever-moving cranes overhead, were rapidly unloading other vessels of miscellaneous commodities. Irish, Negro, Chinese, and Malay porters were running here and there; cabs and carts were driving about, and other persons on foot and on horseback, mostly in a hurry, evidently with business on their hands. There were, however, a few saunterers, and they were either almost naked black aborigines, with lank hair, hideous countenances, and thin legs, or men with their hands in their pockets, in threadbare coats and uncleaned shoes, their countenances pale and dejected, and mostly marked by intemperance. Many of them were young, but there were some of all ages—broken-down gentlemen, unprepared for colonial life, without energy or perseverance, unable and still oftener unwilling to work. The brothers had not to inquire who they were. Their history was written on their foreheads.

W. H. G. Kingston

"What shall we do next?" asked Arthur.

"I should like to get out of this place as soon as possible."

"So should I, indeed," said James; "but we must go to an inn for the night, ascertain where labour is most wanted in the interior, and how best to find our way there."

"You and I can scarcely carry our traps any way up those streets; perhaps one or two of those poor fellows there would like to earn a shilling by helping us," said Arthur, beckoning to some of the above-mentioned idlers.

The first summoned walked away without noticing them, another stared, a third exclaimed, "Egregious snob! what can he want?" and a fourth walked up with his fists doubled, crying out in a furious tone, "How do you dare to make faces at me, you young scoundrel?"

"Pardon me, sir," said James, quietly; "my brother made no faces at you. We merely thought that you might be willing to assist in carrying our luggage."

"I assist you in carrying your luggage! A good joke! But I see you are not quite what I took you for; and if you'll stand a nobbler or two, I don't mind calling a porter for you, and showing you to a slap-up inn to suit you," said the man, his manner completely changing. "You'll have to pay the porter pretty handsomely, my new chums! People don't work for nothing in this country."

While they were hesitating about accepting the man's offer to get a porter, thinking that there could be no harm in that, a country lad, Sam Green by name, who had come out as a steerage passenger with them, approached. As soon as he saw them he ran up exclaiming—

"Oh, Master Gilpins, there's a chap been and run off wi' all my traps, and I've not a rag left, but just what I stand in!"

Sam was, of course, glad enough to assist in carrying their luggage. James apologised to the stranger, saying he would not trouble him.

"Not so fast, young chum!" exclaimed the man. "You promised me a couple of nobblers, and engaged me to call a porter. I'm not going to let you off so easily! Down with the tin, or come and stand the treat!"

The Gilpins were rather more inclined to laugh at the man than to be angry; certainly they had no intention of paying him. Perhaps their looks expressed this. He was becoming more and more blustering, when a cry from several people was heard; and looking up the street, an open carriage with a pair of horses was seen dashing down towards the water at a furious rate. There was no coachman on the box, but that there was some one in the carriage James discovered by seeing a shawl fluttering from the side, and by hearing a piercing shriek, uttered apparently as if then, for the first time, the lady had discovered the imminence of her danger. In a few seconds the carriage would have been dragged over the quay and into water many fathoms deep.

"Stop the horses! Fifty—a hundred—five hundred pounds to whoever will do it!" shouted a man's voice from within.

Right and left the people were flying out of the way of the infuriated steeds. There was not manhood enough left apparently in the idle, dissipated-looking loiterers who were standing near. Two or three took their hands out of their pockets and ran forward, but quickly returned as the horses came galloping by them. The young Gilpins heard the gentleman's offer.

W. H. G. Kingston

"We don't want that!" cried James. "Come on, Arthur!"

They sprang towards the carriage, one on each side; and then turning, ran in the direction it was going, grasping the head-stalls of the animals as they passed, but allowing themselves to be carried on some way, their weight however telling instantly on the galloping steeds.

Sam Green had remained standing by the luggage, having made up his mind that the suspicious-looking stranger would decamp with it, if left unguarded. When, however, he saw that the horses, in spite of his young friends' efforts, would drag the carriage over, unless stopped, he started up, with his hands outstretched before him, uttering with stentorian voice a true English "Woh! woho!" and then, with an arm from which an ox would dislike to receive a blow, he seized the heads of the horses, already trying to stop themselves, and forced them back from the edge stones of the quay, which they had almost reached. Undoubtedly the horses had been broken in by a trainer from the old country: Sam Green's "Woh! woho!" acted like magic; and the pacified though trembling animals allowed themselves to be turned round, with their heads away from the water. While the elder Gilpin and Sam held them, Arthur ran to open the door, that the lady and gentleman might alight. The one was of middle age, the other very young—father and daughter, Arthur surmised.

"My brave lads, you have nobly won the reward I promised," said the gentleman, as he lifted out his daughter, who, pale and agitated, still, by the expression of her countenance, showed the gratitude she felt.

"I am sure that my brother and I require no reward for doing our duty," answered Arthur, blushing as he spoke. "Besides, without the aid of that other lad, our fellow-passenger, we should probably have failed."

"What! I took you for labouring youths, I beg your pardon," said the gentleman, giving a glance of surprise at him.

"Our intention is to labour," said Arthur, unaffectedly.

"Ah! you have the stuff in you to command success," said the gentleman. "But I must request you to accompany me for a short distance, as my daughter prefers walking; and if I once lose sight of you in this straggling city, I may not easily find you again."

"Thank you, sir," said Arthur; "we have our luggage with us, and must go to an inn; but if you will favour me with your address, we will call on you before we leave Sydney."

While they were speaking, the coachman, in consequence of whose carelessness in letting go their heads the horses had run away, came up, and released James and Sam. Not a word of scolding was uttered—the gentleman thought a moment.

"Here, Sykes, lift that luggage into the carriage, and drive these young gentleman home; leave them there, and come back for Miss Fanny and me to the club."

In vain the young Gilpins expostulated.

"I am a determined person, and will have it so," said the gentleman.

Before they looked round, Sam had stowed away their luggage in the carriage, greatly to the disappointment of the bully, who had, it seemed, been watching for an opportunity to make off with a portion. The stranger then, almost against their will, forced them into it; and writing a few lines on the leaf of a pocket-book, gave it to the coachman. "Come, my friend, you must go in also," he added, taking Sam by

W. H. G. Kingston

the arm.

Sam drew back, and, touching his hat, exclaimed, "Noa, sir—noa, thank ye. It 'ud ne'er do for me to ride wi' the young squires; I know my place better nor that."

A mob such as Sydney, of all British ports, perhaps, can alone produce, had by this time collected round the carriage. Sam's remark produced a loud guffaw laugh from among them, and a variety of observations came rattling down on him, such as "Go it, young Touch-my-hat; the nob will pay you—he's a nigger with a white face. I wonder where he was raised? His mother was a dancing mistress—little doubt of that."

Sam's temper had been irritated from the loss of his property, which he very naturally concluded had been stolen by some of his tormentors. He now looked as if he were going to give way to his temper. Instead of so doing, however, he turned calmly round with his double fist, and said slowly, "I'll tell you what, young chaps, a man who respects himself keeps his own place, and when he meets a gentleman he'd think himself without manners nor character if he didn't touch his hat to him. Did any on ye ever see two gentlemen take off their hats to each other? Well, then, I have; and I should just like to know which was the worst man of the two? I'll say another thing—I have mostly found that when I have took my hat off to a gentleman he took his off to me; and I wonder if his friends laughed at him. But I suppose some of you are great nobs yourselves, and know all about what nobs do."

Having thus delivered himself, Sam, giving a contemptuous glance at his opponents, slowly mounted the box by the side of the coachman. The gentleman, who had walked on with his daughter, bowed to the Gilpins as they passed.

"I am afraid that, from taking us to be ploughboys, he now believes we are young noblemen in disguise," observed Arthur. "This is a very different style to that in which we could have expected to have entered Sydney half an hour ago."

"Perhaps he thinks more of the service we have rendered him than we should," answered his brother; "however, it's a curious adventure, certainly."

"Well, muster, there be rum jokes in this town o' yours," observed Sam to the coachman, after keeping silence for some time.

"There be, young man," was the laconic answer; "and rum things done."

In this Sam agreed, informing Mr Sykes—for this, he ascertained, was the coachman's name—how he had lost his property.

"Be thou the young man who stopped the 'osses?" inquired Sykes.

"The young squires did it, and I helped 'em," said Sam.

"And saved my bacon," observed Sykes.

"I say, Muster Sykes, what's the gen'l'man's name?" asked Sam, discovering, perhaps, by the tone of the coachman's voice, rather than by any perceptible change in his mask-like features, that he was not ill disposed towards him, and preparing therefore to be confidential.

Sykes informed him that his master's name was Prentiss, that he was a large squatter, that there were other brothers all well off, and an old father; and that, take him all in all as masters went, he was not a bad one. Sam, in return, told him all about himself, and all he knew about the Gilpins, by which time the carriage had reached the door of Mr Prentiss's residence, in one of the best parts of Sydney. It was a handsome house; and a respectable-looking servant-woman, after a few words from the coachman, showed the Gilpins into a well-furnished dining-room, their luggage being placed in the hall.

"You'll go with me, young man," observed Mr Sykes to Sam; "you'll be more comfortable than with the gentry."

To this Sam agreed; and drove round to the back of the house, where he was introduced to Mrs Sykes, who lived over the coach-house, and numerous Masters and Misses Sykes, thin, sallow, and remarkably precocious young people, the eldest not being more than ten. Among this hopeful family Sam in a few minutes made himself a great favourite.

The young immigrants waited the arrival of their host with no little curiosity, for they knew less of him than Sam had contrived to learn. In a short time, however, the servant, placing a tray with meat, bread, fruit, and light wine, begged them to refresh themselves. This occupied their time till the arrival of Mr Prentiss. Perhaps James was disappointed at not seeing the young lady when her father entered the room. Mr Prentiss put out his hand, cordially welcoming them to Australia and to his house; and, begging them to make it their home during their stay, he quickly drew out from them a statement of their plans and wishes. "You can make a fair start," he observed. "You have the five hundred pounds I promised, very nobly won, too; and I may give you a few hints besides as to the purchase of stock. You will, of course, become squatters—by far the best business for young men of enterprise and activity. What do you say to it?"

"We should like nothing better, sir," answered James. "But— I speak again for my brother as well as for myself—we cannot accept payment for performing a mere act of duty; your advice and assistance may be of the greatest value to us, and of that we will gladly avail ourselves. The young man who helped us to stop the horses must, of course, speak for himself."

"Well, well, I admire your independence and high feeling," answered Mr Prentiss. "I doubt, however, that you will find many in this country to consider that you are right; but perhaps I may be of service to you in the way you desire. You, of course, will make my house your home while you remain in Sydney; when you wish to commence your life in the bush, I will send you up the country to my father and some brothers of mine, who will put you in the way of a fair start. Your young shipmate fairly earned a portion of the reward; he also deserves my gratitude. He looks as if there was work in him, and to such a person I can be permanently of use. Unhappily, numbers of men come out here—they may be counted by hundreds or thousands—who will not work, or who cannot work; nothing suits them. They come with pockets full of letters, expecting first-rate situations with nothing to do. How can such people be assisted to any advantage? Give them money, and they squander it; place them in situations of trust, and they are dismissed as incompetent, or they throw them up as uncongenial to their tastes. All we want in this magnificent country are people who will try to work, and if they do not succeed in one thing, will turn their hands to something else. There is ample room, I say, for persons of every possible description, provided always that they belong to the 'try' school."

Mr Prentiss insisted on taking his guests round the town to

W. H. G. Kingston

visit its lions; and greatly surprised they were to see the wonderful progress it had already made. "Wool has done it all! Well may the golden fleece be our emblem!" he observed.

At the late dinner hour they were introduced to Mrs Prentiss and two daughters—the young lady they had before seen and a younger sister. All awkwardness soon wore off, and they felt themselves perfectly at home. Mr Prentiss had a conversation with Sam, the result of which made him supremely happy; his satisfaction was not decreased either when, two days afterwards, Sykes brought him his bag of clothes.

"Don't ask questions, young man," he observed, as he handed them; "there are few of the old hands I don't know, and I guessed who had your property."

Pleasant as the two young Gilpins found their stay in Sydney, they did not disguise their anxiety to be off into the country; and their new friend accordingly made arrangements for their journey.

CHAPTER TWO

A dray, similar in construction to that used by brewers in England, but drawn by oxen, and laden with all sorts of stores, such as are required on an Australian farm—tea, carpenters' tools and agricultural implements, groceries and casks of liquor, clothing and furniture—was making its way towards the north-east from Sydney. There was the bullock-driver in charge, with his chum, a newly hired hand, and Sam Green, who walked or sat on the dray; while the two Gilpins rode alongside on horses, provided by Mr Prentiss. They were dressed more in the Australian style than when they landed, and in a way much better suited to the climate. The road had been excellent for a hundred miles or more, with numerous villages near it, and a large proportion of houses of entertainment, so that they had no want of accommodation when they halted. They had now for some time left the high-road, and though there were inns, and occasionally villages, and farms, and stock stations, they had sometimes to depend on their own resources, and to bivouac in the bush. This the young immigrants found by far the pleasantest part of their journey. The oxen were turned loose to graze at leisure; sticks were collected, and a fire lighted for boiling the tea-kettle and cooking the damper. The old hands troubled themselves very little about their night's lodging; they, like Sam Green, were satisfied with the bare ground under the dray if it threatened rain, or anywhere near

W. H. G. Kingston

it if the weather was fine. A small tent had been provided by Mr Prentiss, which, with some ticking filled with dry grass, gave the Gilpins a luxurious lodging for the night. They could scarcely go to sleep on turning in for their first real night in the bush, from the novelty of the scene and the prospects opening up to them. Before dawn they both started up, awoke by the strangest and most discordant sounds.

"What can it be?" cried James.

"An attack of the blacks," said Arthur, rubbing his eyes. "But no! Listen! They are birds, I verily believe; but the strangest birds I ever heard."

He was right: there was the hideous, unearthly cry of the laughing-jackass, called often the bushman's clock; the screaming cry of thousands of parrots flying here and there through the forest; there was the cackle of the wattle-bird, the clear notes of the magpie, and the confused chattering of thousands of leather-heads; while many other birds added their notes to the discordant chorus, and speedily banished sleep from the eyes of their hearers. The stockmen started to their feet, and hurried off to bring in the oxen and horses; a fire was lighted, tea boiled, breakfast discussed with considerable rapidity; and, before the sun was up, the party had recommenced their journey along the dusty dray-track— for as yet it deserved that name rather than a road. The scenery was varied, and often very beautiful when viewed under a clear blue sky and bright sun. The beds of streams were frequently passed, but they were either dry altogether, or occasional holes only with water in them could be seen here and there along the course, or, if nowhere dry, they were easily forded. The Irish bullock-driver, Larry Killock, told Sam that, in the rainy season, these were often foaming torrents, rushing on with terrific noise, and sweeping away everything they meet.

"Many a poor fellow has been drowned in trying to cross on horseback where, perhaps, he went over with dry feet a few days before," said Larry.

"That's after the snow melts," observed Sam.

"Snow! man alive! It's a small matter of snow comes down from the sky in this beautiful country, except, now and then, on the top of the Blue Mountains out there; though, as for frosts, it's cold enough on the high ground in July and August, when the south wind blows, to make a fellow blow his fingers to keep them warm, and to think a blazing fire and a blanket pleasant companions."

Sam thought that Larry was quizzing him, but still he did not like to accuse him directly. "It's a strange country this, then, muster, I'm thinking," he remarked cautiously.

"Strange! It is a strange country, faith!" answered Larry. "It is summer here when, by all dacent rules, it should be winter; the south wind is cold, and the north blazing hot. There are creatures with four legs which have ducks' heads; and birds, with long legs and no wings, as tall as horses; while some of the animals stow their young away in a bag in front of them, instead of letting them follow properly at their heels, as pigs and ducks and hens do in the old country. The trees shed their bark instead of their leaves; and it's only just surprising to me that the people walk on their feet instead of their heads, and that the sun thinks fit to rise in the east instead of the west; and it's often when I wake in the mornin' that I look out expecting to see that he's grown tired of his old ways, and changed to suit the other things in the land."

Sam, who could appreciate an English style of joke, was unable to make out whether or not the Irishman was in earnest; but he thought it wise to wait till he could learn the

W. H. G. Kingston

truth from his young friends, when they camped in the evening.

"It's only just come out, ye are?" asked Larry.

Sam told him all about himself, as he had told Sykes, expecting an equal amount of communicativeness in return. "You've been some time in the country, master, I'm thinking? How did you come out?"

Larry looked at him with a twinkle in his eye. "Faith, that's just a sacret between myself and them who knows all about it," he answered, with a laugh. "It's my belief that the big-wigs across the fish-pond had just an idea of the mighty great value I'd be to the country, and sent me out free of all charge to myself and family intirely."

The scenery improved as the travellers advanced, and contrasted favourably with the dusty, stony, and worn-out region through which they had passed nearer the capital.

"Horrible farming!" observed James; "if such were practised in England universally, the whole country would become a desert in a few years."

Sometimes they passed through scenery like that of a park in England, with open green pastures sprinkled with clumps of trees; some deserving the names of woods, others consisting but of a few trees. The greater number were *Eucalypti* the evergreen gum, and stringy-bark trees; but on the banks of streams and on the hillsides, and sometimes in rich, alluvial valleys, such as are found in the northern hemisphere and in less sunny climes, were to be seen flowers, of great size and beauty, such as flourish only in greenhouses in England; while a great variety of the orchis tribe, and geraniums, both large and small, were found in great profusion. The trees, the names of many of which were given by Larry, bore little or no resemblance to those of the same name at home. Among the most common were the box, wattle, and cherry; but undoubtedly the most prominent everywhere in the landscape were the old gum trees, and the huge iron stringy-bark trees, which, now with shattered and weird appearance, had braved the fierce storms of winter and the hot blasts of summer for centuries. Many strange birds flew by overhead, and still stranger wild animals started up from beneath some sheltering bush, and ran off along the fresh glades, all reminding the new-comers how far distant they were from the home of their childhood.

The old settled district had been left far behind before the animal they most wished to see started up near them. He was a large creature, full five feet in height as he sat upright under the scant shade of a venerable gum tree, contemplating apparently the scene before him. His long tail was stretched out on the ground behind him—an important support, and his little fore-paws tucked up in front. James and Arthur were ahead of their party, and so quietly had their horses trod over the soft ground that he did not appear to have heard them. They possessed guns, parting gifts from Mr Prentiss; but, not being required as a means of defence or offence, they had been left in the dray. The kangaroo ("an old man" Larry called him) at length, hearing a sound, turned his mild, intelligent countenance towards them, and as he did so instantly gave a spring forward, startling them by its suddenness and the extent of ground it cleared. Away he went, moving with similar springs, at a rate fleet as that of the deer. In vain Larry and the men with the dray shouted and ran after him with their guns. He was out of range before they could lift them to their shoulders. Larry said that possibly a mob might be come upon before long. In another hour or so, as they were travelling along a somewhat stony ridge, a large number of creatures were seen in the fertile

W. H. G. Kingston

valley below them. Some were lying stretched at length on their sides, some were frisking about, round and over each other, and others were sitting up, sedately watching the rest.

"Hurra, now! There's the mob I told you of!" shouted Larry. "If we had but the dogs and the master's rifle, we'd have more kangaroo steaks for supper than we'd eat in a week."

He could scarcely restrain himself from leaving his bullocks and giving chase; he made a start indeed, but checked himself in time, seeing that the probable result would have been the upsetting of his dray and the destruction of most of its cargo. The young Gilpins with Sam found their way down the hill, hoping to ride down one of them; but the quick scent and keen eyes of the animals discovered their approach, and in an instant all were up on their feet and tails ready for a start—the mothers picking up the young joeys and putting them into their pouches—and off went the entire herd down the valley, springing along in the most curious fashion, till they were out of sight.

Sam Green's open eyes of astonishment were very amusing. "Well! I always did think that animals had four legs, and there they go just two and a tail, a-skipping like grasshoppers over the ground. Well, well, well!" he continued ejaculating till they disappeared. "There they go; there they go! There's nothing I won't believe after that!"

Their adventures as they travelled on were to be singularly few, they thought. Now a dingo or wild dog, now a toombat or opossum, made its appearance, and created matter of interest and inquiry. One evening, after they had camped on the borders of a wide plain, containing fine sheep-runs, which they were to cross the next day, the brothers led on their horses to find better feed than appeared near at hand; and, having tethered them, they sat down to talk over the future, and to commune with themselves. Their heads had been resting on their hands for some time, when Arthur, looking up, saw a creature approaching from a distance. That it was an emu they guessed at once. They sat still, afraid of frightening it away. It stalked leisurely on towards their horses, not noticing them. Its head seemed fully six feet from the ground, at the end of a long neck; its legs were thick, to support its fat, tub-shaped body, of a brownish-black colour. Reaching the horses, it stopped, made a curious noise, which sounded like "Boo!" in their faces, and which caused them to start back. James and Arthur, thinking that their steeds would have broken their tethers, jumped up, when the emu, having satisfied his curiosity, turned round and trotted off, at a pace which showed that he had no fear of being pursued.

Towards the close of the day the travellers, after crossing an elevated down, saw before them a silvery stream running through a wide valley towards the east, its banks fringed by a variety of trees; while not far from them, amid a grove of fruit trees, appeared a pretty dwelling-house, with a verandah running round it, and near at hand, barns, sheds, stables, and other outhouses. A closer inspection showed them that there were carpenters' and blacksmiths shops; indeed, it was a complete farm establishment on a large scale.

As riding on, in advance of the dray, they reached the door, a stout, hearty-looking old gentleman came out to meet them, and welcomed them in the most cordial manner. Their horses were quickly unsaddled and turned into a paddock, and they themselves conducted into the house, and introduced to the members of the family as late arrivals from the old country. All welcomed them; and they were soon seated at a well-covered supper-table, surrounded by the various inmates of the house. The young strangers were surprised to find that the letter of introduction they brought had not been read, and that the kindness they were receiving was quite independent

W. H. G. Kingston

of anything that might be said in their favour. It was not till the next day that the old Mr Prentiss alluded to it. "We received you, young gentlemen, as strangers," he remarked; "but I little thought how much I owed you for saving from injury, if not death, those so dear to me."

James and Arthur Gilpin agreed that their "lines had fallen to them in pleasant places." They were treated as members of the family, and, what was of the greatest consequence to them as intending settlers, they were shown all the operations taking place on the farm. As they gave diligent attention to everything they saw, they rapidly acquired a sufficient knowledge of agriculture and of the management of sheep and cattle, as practised in Australia, to enable them, with their previous experience as farmers in England, to commence farming on their own account.

While, however, they were in search of a station to suit them, Mr Prentiss received an application to find a gentleman capable of taking the management of a sheep and cattle farm, about a hundred and fifty miles off. "Quite in our neighbourhood, as we measure distances in this country," he remarked. He proposed to the young Gilpins that they should accept the post. "You will be allowed to keep a proportion of sheep and cattle on your own account, and receive wages for looking after those of your employer, so that you will gain in both ways. You will find also an established system by which, if it prove a good one, time and labour may be saved. I would gladly find you employment, but this will be far more to your advantage. It was hoped, I believe, that one of my own sons would take it."

The brothers at once agreed to accept the offer.

CHAPTER THREE

The Gilpins no longer felt like newly arrived immigrants when they found themselves on their way to Warragong, the station of which they had undertaken charge. They were far, however, from being over-confident of success, or of pleasing their employers; but they had resolved to make up by diligence and perseverance for their want of experience, and Mr Prentiss assured them that he had no doubt of their doing well. Sam Green had thrown in his lot with them, and though receiving good wages from Mr Prentiss, he begged that he might be allowed to accompany them on the chance of their being able to give him permanent employment. Knowing by this time the value of a thoroughly trustworthy servant in Australia, they were very glad to accept his offer. They, as well as Sam, had been furnished with excellent horses; and, much to his own satisfaction as well as theirs, Larry Killock was sent with a light cart to convey their luggage and various luxuries, which had been provided through the kindness of Mrs Prentiss. A native black, partly civilised, and able to speak broken English, accompanied them as guide, and formed the fifth person of this party. He either travelled in the cart or ran on foot beside it.

"I should think that very few settlers begin a life in the bush with so many advantages as we possess," observed Arthur, as he rode on with his brother, a little ahead of the cart; "we appear to have jumped over all difficulties, and to have arrived at a point which many only reach after years of toil."

"I am not quite certain that it will prove to our permanent advantage," answered James. "I would rather have begun as we proposed, and worked our way upward; we should the better be able to encounter difficulties or mishaps which may occur."

"Well, I vote we do not grumble with our good fortune," said Arthur, laughing; "we shall have plenty to do, depend on that."

There was no great variety of scenery in that part of the country over which they travelled, but for the want of it the beauty of the climate, and the sense of present freedom which they enjoyed, made ample amends. Without luggage they might have performed the journey in three days, but with the cart, twenty or, at the most, thirty miles could not be got over in the day. Even supposing that they could have found their way alone, it would not have been altogether safe to leave the cart without protection. Bushrangers were occasionally, though rarely, heard of, and would probably, if they fell in with the cart, make no scruple of running off with it, and perhaps murder the driver. Any wandering blacks from the interior might also pillage the cart, and most probably kill poor Larry.

Larry had been entertaining Sam Green with an account of the depredations committed by such gentry in the bygone days of the colony, when the Dick Turpins, who had obtained a short-lived celebrity on the highway of Old England, laid the settlers in this new land under contribution; and the white stockmen shot down the black natives with as little compunction as they would kangaroos; the blacks, in retaliation, murdering them or any white men they could meet with. Larry, observing the wide-mouthed interest created by his narratives, went on till poor Sam began to wish himself safe out of the country again. They were crossing a wide plain, with a light soil thickly covered with grass. A cloud of dust was seen to the right of the direction in which they were travelling; it increased in extent, and rose higher and higher.

"Be them the niggers coming to murder us?" asked Sam, in a fright.

"If them are niggers, they're big ones, my boy, anyhow," answered Larry, evasively.

A dull, regular, pounding sound was heard, and at length dark forms were seen issuing from the cloud of dust—a few first, and then more and more, resolving themselves into bullocks, black, white, and dun, galloping on and bellowing with might and main. Horsemen appeared on either side, like officers on a parade, and with their long whips, which they kept on cracking like pistol-shots, they kept order among their unruly charge. Shouting and shrieking, they galloped round from the rear to the side to bring back any beast which showed an intention of straying away, their dogs sagaciously rendering them assistance by barking at the heels of the animals, and turning them back into the herd. What with the thunder-like bellowing of the cattle and the tramp of their feet, the shouting of the drivers, the cracking of their whips, the barking of the dogs, the dust from the ground, and the steam from the creatures' backs, as, lashing their long tails, they tore onwards, jostling each other in their course, their sharp horns lowered for the charge, the approaching herd appeared like some vast army of savage monsters, rushing on to meet their foes in battle. To draw up out of their way was impossible, and the travellers soon found themselves surrounded by the herd; the creatures, however, turned their horns aside, while the shape of their own heads and the width of their backs prevented them from running them into their companions in front or on either side, in spite of the seemingly confused way in which they were hurrying on. The herd had passed, when two of the principal drivers, who, in spite of their rough dress and hair-covered countenances, appeared to be gentlemen, drew up and saluted the Gilpins with "Good day, friends; whither bound?"

"To Warragong, to take charge of the station," said James.

"I wish you joy," remarked one of the strangers; "you will have no easy task, I take it. A sad scoundrel has had the management of it for some time, as we know to our cost, having once employed him. I am afraid, also, from the sort of men he always gets about him, that you will have no small trouble with them." The strangers informed them that they were bound south to the Port Philip district, where there was a great demand for cattle.

As the evening was approaching, the parties agreed to camp together. Fires were lighted, the triangles erected, and the pots were soon boiling, while the quickly made damper was placed under the ashes to bake for the coming meal. None of the party, however, could keep their seats by the fire long, without being often summoned to their feet, and sometimes to their saddles, to drive in the straying bullocks. It seemed as hard work to keep them together when resting as to drive them forward, but neither master nor men were disconcerted; they rushed here and there with shout and song and laughter, till they had brought back the straying cattle, and then they sat down by the fire, or rolled themselves up in their blankets, as if nothing had happened. The Gilpins were sorry to part from their new friends, whose frank, hearty manners had won their regard. The morning meal of tea, damper, and pork having been discussed, they rode off in opposite directions.

"Not pleasant information this, our friends gave us last night," said Arthur. "What can we do?"

"Wait events," answered his brother; "forewarned is forearmed. We will keep our knowledge to ourselves, though it will be necessary to advise Green not to trust to any of the men, so as to be led into mischief by them. Perhaps the accounts of their misconduct may have been exaggerated."

Travelling in Australia has its disagreeables as well as its agreeables: there are heavy rains and fogs and sharp winds in winter; and in summer, scorching blasts and stifling heat, and biting or stinging insects, flying, and crawling, and hopping, and dust and smoke from bush fires and the burning trees, and want, at times, of water; but, notwithstanding these occasional drawbacks, so delightful is the perfect freedom to be enjoyed, the pure, bright atmosphere, and the general healthfulness of the climate, that in the opinion of most people the advantages very greatly preponderate.

The brothers had expected to reach the station in the afternoon, but an accident to the cart caused some delay, and the sun set before it appeared in sight. Their black guide, however, assured them that the intervening country was tolerably level and easy, and that as there were certain woods he knew well, and a river on the other side, they could not miss their way. Accordingly they pushed on, though it became so dark that they began to wish that they had camped at the usual hour. Suddenly, as they reached the confines of a wood, their horses snorted and started, and refused to proceed—those in the cart very nearly upsetting it by turning rapidly round; and, had not Sam caught their heads, they would have galloped off in an opposite direction. Directly

W. H. G. Kingston

afterwards, a bright light burst forth from the wood and a spectacle appeared sufficient to make even a stout heart, with any tendency to superstitious feelings, tremble. From among the trees, just beyond the light, appeared, flitting in and out, some twenty or thirty blanched skeletons, throwing their bony arms and legs with the greatest rapidity into every conceivable attitude. Now they disappeared in the darkness, now again they darted into light; round and round they went, now seeming to sink into the ground, now leaping into the air, and often turning head over heels. All the time not a sound proceeded from the phantom-looking dancers. The Gilpins could scarcely help fancying themselves under some delusion. They rubbed their eyes.

"What is it?" exclaimed Arthur. "Horrible! most horrible! Do you see the skeletons?"

"Indeed I do," answered his brother; "but such things cannot be—are not—at all events."

Sam Green had hitherto been engaged with the horses; he now came up to the point where the hideous spectacle was visible, and no sooner did his eyes rest on it than he exclaimed, "Run, squires, run! If it was mortal foes I'd stick by ye; but that's more than any mortal man can dare to face. Oh! this is a terrible country, where the people cannot lie quiet in graves, but must needs go skipping about without any flesh on their bones."

"The hoighth of ondacency!" cried out Larry, in a voice which showed very little, if any, alarm. "Murra, go and tell your ugly countrymen that they are frightening the horses, and that they must turn their other sides to us till we have passed."

This order was given to the guide, who ran fearlessly up to

the spot where the skeleton dance was proceeding, and no sooner did he reach it than the whole vanished like magic.

"It's only some black fellows dancing a Corroborry," said the Irishman, laughing; "you needn't be in such a mighty tremble, Sam. We haven't the shred of a ghost out here; there may be some in the old country, but they're not fond of the salt sea, and couldn't cross it, not if they were paid for it, except they came out at the expense of the Government, like some other honest gintlemen I've heard spake of."

The horses, however, were still very unwilling to proceed, and it was some time before they could be coaxed past the suspicious spot; they then set off at increased speed to get away from the object of their dread. The party pulled up for the black, who came running up. "No good people," he said, in a low voice; "come here, do bad."

The Gilpins, hearing his remarks, endeavoured to discover the reason of his supposing that the party of natives they had just passed were badly disposed, but could elicit no further information from him. It was more than an hour after this that a glimmering light appeared ahead, which Murra, the guide, assured them must proceed from the station. It appeared to be somewhat above them on the hillside, and they soon afterwards found themselves ascending slightly towards it. They had not got far, however, before several large dogs flew out, barking furiously, towards them. They and Larry shouted loudly to the hut-keeper to call the animals off, but no one appeared, and, the dogs contenting themselves with barking, they proceeded on to the hut, from the window of which the light gleamed out. The dogs, still loudly barking, at length roused up a couple of rough-looking men, who staggered out of the door, and, one of them holding a lamp, stared stupidly at the travellers, at the

W. H. G. Kingston

same time that, with loud oaths, he shouted to the dogs to be quiet.

"Oh! you are strangers," said the least tipsy; "well, you shall have a stranger's welcome in the bush; and so you may just go and turn out your horses, and then come and get what you can inside."

"We've come to take charge of the station," said James, rather nettled; "so, my men, I rather think that it is your duty to see and make yourselves useful to us."

"Ho! ho! Pretty sort of masters you'd make over us!" cried the man, holding up the light in their faces. "To my mind, you'd better go back to them that sent you."

This was even a worse reception than they had expected; but, perceiving that the man was very drunk, they saw that it would not be wise to irritate him.

"Well, my man," said James, calmly, "we have pushed on here in the hopes of being welcomed, but all we will ask now is a supper and a night's rest."

"As you speak us fair, we'll treat you fair, whoever you may be," said the man. "Come in; the kettle is boiling, and there's a damper or two ready under the ashes."

The cart having been placed close to the hut, the horses were unharnessed and unsaddled and turned out to pick up their supper, and the whole party were soon collected in the hut. The interior showed evident signs of a late debauch. There was a rough table in the centre covered with tobacco-ashes, a broken black cutty, or pipe, some battered tin mugs, and a couple of empty spirit bottles on their sides, while under it lay a couple of men fast asleep, and another in the corner.

Some kicks from the shoe of their more sober companion, who had brought the newly arrived party in, roused them up; and he then proceeded to eject them, telling them to go to Bateman's hut, where they would find shelter. Grumbling, they staggered out, except two, who were too far gone to move. The hut was, as might have been expected, in a very dirty and untidy condition—so dirty, indeed, that the Gilpins were contemplating camping outside, when Larry, going out, reported that a storm was brewing, and proceeded forthwith to bring the contents of the cart inside. A plentiful though roughly cooked supper was soon on the table to which all hands did ample justice. The hut was a long, narrow building, with the entrance door towards one end, where the mud-built fireplace was formed and the table stood. In the further end were some bunks, or standing bed-places, and the stores were piled up. Larry placed the articles he had brought in the cart across the hut, so as more effectually to screen off the inner end. He and the hut-keeper, whom he addressed as Jonas Knoll, appeared to be old acquaintances, but very few words passed between them. For the first time since they had landed, the Gilpins lay down to rest with a feeling that they were not as safe as they would have been in their own home in England.

Before Larry lay down, after the hut-keeper had gone to sleep, they observed that he put fresh grease into the lamp and trimmed the wick. More than once James awoke and looked around; everybody in the hut appeared to be sleeping soundly. The two stockmen and the hut-keeper especially were snoring loudly, and not a sound from the outside was heard. "It is wrong to be giving way to fear," he said to himself. "These coarse fellows have been indulging, according to their tastes, in a debauch, and were annoyed at being interrupted. They would scarcely dare to harm us even if they wished it. We must keep a tight rein on them and a careful watch on their proceedings, without allowing them to

W. H. G. Kingston

discover that they are especially observed, and we shall do well."

The next morning the hut-keepers and stockmen belonging to the headquarters of the station made their appearance, sobered, and tolerably respectful in their manner; though there was an expression in their eyes and a tone in their voices which made the young managers believe that it would take but little to make them break out into open mutiny. They were, however, surprised at Larry's changed manner. There was an impudent swagger in all he did, and when ordered to perform any duty, he invariably replied in a way which made his companions laugh, though he executed the order with promptness. He seemed to be on familiar terms with all the people on the station, and to be a favourite among them. The brothers at once saw that there was much to do, and many alterations to be made in every direction about the station. The huts were in a dilapidated condition— the one intended for their residence was so dirty as to be scarcely habitable; the stock-yards required repair; and, worse than all, the books were so badly kept that it was almost impossible to ascertain the number and state of the stock, either of cattle, sheep, or horses, or of the stores. The overseer was absent—gone to a distant run—so they took possession of the books, which had been left carelessly out, with the intention of verifying them with the actual state of things. Having made the necessary extracts, they locked them up and started on horseback, accompanied by Sam, whose practised eye was likely to prove of great assistance in numbering the flocks of sheep and herds of cattle which were to be inspected. They had not made their intention known, and, just as they were starting, they summoned the most civil-looking of the stockmen, and ordered him to mount his horse and accompany them as a guide. As every flock is named, they had no difficulty in indicating the flock they wished to visit; but they did not tell him till they had got some way from the station, so that he would have no opportunity of communicating with his companions should he suspect their designs. Arrived at a run, they immediately called the shepherd, and ordered him to make his flock pass before them, when they took careful note of their numbers, appearance, and general condition. Having done so, they put spurs to their horses and galloped off to the next run. As they had a pocket compass and had been furnished with a rough map of the country, they had no difficulty in assuring themselves that their guide was conducting them aright. The shepherds and stock-keepers looked puzzled, and as not a single remark of approval or disapproval was uttered, they could not make up their minds how to proceed. Several of them would have given much to peep into the notebook which those quiet-looking young men held in their hands. Refreshing themselves and their steeds at a stock-keeper's hut, they returned home late in the evening, satisfied that a large amount of rascality had been going forward, and that it would require great judgment and determination on their part to put matters to right. The next day and the following were employed in the same manner. Each day confirmed them more and more in their opinion. For the present, however, they could only watch the proceedings of the men under them. They could not dismiss the whole of them, nor could they ascertain who were the most guilty. That the overseer was a great scoundrel they had no doubt, and they therefore agreed that he must at once be got rid of. James had written an account of the state of things to Mr Prentiss, but doubted whether to entrust it to Larry Killock, who had so completely identified himself with the other men, that they thought it probable he might give it to them to read, and so put them on their guard. They were still in this state of doubt when the time arrived for Larry to take his departure. They were sitting in the hut at supper, the work of the day over, no one but Sam being near, when the Irishman put his head in at the door. Looking round, and assuring himself that they were the

W. H. G. Kingston

only occupants of the building, he approached them with his former civil manner.

"It's all pretence, yer honours," he whispered, with his hand to his nose. "They're big rascals, every mother's son of them; and I'd give my right hand to be allowed to stop, if I thought that they'd be doing you any mischief; but I don't think they'll dare to work you harm. The worst of them hasn't come yet, and when he does, he'll try to make you believe that he's the most honest man alive. But, whist, there's some one coming. If you'd have the goodness to kick me out of the hut, and call me an impudent thief of the world, it would keep up appearances."

The brothers heartily thanked the Irishman; but were not obliged to fulfil his last request, as he managed to run out of the hut before any one appeared. The following evening, while they were sitting as before, at supper, a horse's hoofs were heard approaching, and soon afterwards a man of middle age, dressed in the usual rough costume of the bush, unceremoniously entered the hut, and, eyeing them with a scrutinising glance, drew up a stool and seated himself at the table.

"The new managers, I presume, Mr—I beg your pardon—I forget your name," he began, in a supercilious tone. "You have stolen a march on me, and I conclude that I am to be superseded."

"That probably will not rest with us," said James. "I suppose that if the trustees of the property find that we can manage it to their satisfaction without help, they will not consider themselves justified in retaining your services."

The overseer, Mr Basham, as he was called, was very unlike the person they expected to see. The shape of his features was remarkably good, though the expression was unsatisfactory; his figure was light and wiry, and capable of enduring considerable fatigue; and his manners were those of a gentleman, marred somewhat by rough companions and the hard life he had led. He saw at once that the young men with whom he had to deal, though inferior to him in knowledge of the world, possessed an uprightness and firmness of character with which he could not trifle. He would much have liked to have entrapped them by offering them a share of his profits, but that plan, it was evident, would not answer with them. Still he trusted that some way might be found of securing what he had obtained, if not for making more.

"Well, well, gentlemen, I have always been an unfortunate person, and so we'll drop the subject, and discuss what is taking place in the great world."

Without more ado he did turn the subject, and showed that he was a man of considerable information, and had received a superior education. This only made him the more difficult to deal with. Though he was now free, they suspected strongly that he had been a convict. They could scarcely believe that with his abilities he would not otherwise have been employed in some higher position. After their inspection of the runs, they had been engaged for a day in turning everything out of the hut, and in having it thoroughly cleansed. They then re-arranged the furniture and contents, according to their own taste. For several days after Mr Basham's return they saw him hunting about the hut in search of something, and at last he asked them if they had seen his books. James at once replied that he had, according to the direction of the trustees, taken possession of them, and should keep them till he received directions to the contrary. He shrugged his shoulders as he observed, "My hard fate again! And so, I suppose, if anything goes wrong, those books are to be brought as evidence against me, though I may be as innocent as the babe unborn." There was a sinister expression in his countenance as he spoke, of which he was probably unaware, but which convinced the young managers that they must be careful how they dealt with him till they could receive authority from Sydney to dismiss him.

In spite of all their vigilance and activity, things continued to go on wrong. Sheep disappeared, carried off by dingoes, or by the native blacks; the shepherds asserted that cattle strayed, and could not be recovered; and two valuable horses, intended to be sent to Sydney, for shipment to India, were missing. More than once the brothers were inclined to wish that they had commenced as squatters on their own account in a small way, with only a few honest men around them; yet, having undertaken their present task, they were not the men to shrink from it. They came to the determination, however, not to embark any of their own small capital till they had got everything to rights, and men under them in whom they could place confidence. At length the looked-for authority arrived to dismiss, not only Mr Basham, but any of the men who might behave ill, or be suspected of malpractices; it being suggested that, as trustworthy men were difficult to procure, it would be injudicious to proceed on light grounds, at the same time, as proof positive would in many cases be impossible, it would not be necessary to wait till it was found. This was throwing a large amount of responsibility on their shoulders, but they determined to do their duty. Mr Basham received his dismissal with great coolness; but again his features assumed the expression the Gilpins had before observed. He claimed as his own a couple of fine horses, and, placing his personal property on one of these and bestriding the other, early the next morning he rode off, the last glance of his cold, grey eye leaving an impression which for many a day remained fixed on the minds of the brothers.

CHAPTER FOUR

The Gilpins found that the superintendence of a large station did not afford a bed of roses. All day long they were in the saddle, overlooking twenty stockmen and shepherds, examining the herds and flocks, and often themselves doctoring any which were found diseased or injured. This they were obliged to do, in consequence of the ignorance or carelessness of the people in charge of them. These, with few exceptions, had been convicts. Of those who had been convicts, some were still working out their sentences with tickets-of-leave, while others, who were free to go where they liked, were too old and destitute of energy to venture on a change of occupation, and remained as before, hut-keepers or shepherds. At each inferior station there was a hut with a hut-keeper, whose duty was to look after the hut, to cook the provisions, and to tend the sheep or cattle brought for any special purpose into the fold or pen. The office was usually held by some old convict or other person unfit for hard labour. Though occasionally there is enough to do, it is considered an idle, lazy life.

The brothers often rode together to the stations, to assist each other; but they had lately, for the sake of covering more ground in the course of the day, taken separate districts, that the stockmen might be kept constantly on the alert, not knowing any moment when the active young managers

W. H. G. Kingston

might pay them a visit. Notwithstanding this, cattle and sheep continued to disappear as before, and they came to the resolution of making every man responsible who lost an animal, and stopping his wages till it was replaced. One day, after a hard morning's work, Arthur Gilpin found himself approaching the rear of a hut, on an out station, at the extreme end of the territory over which the cattle ranged— the whole being considerably larger than many a German principality. The ground was soft, and his horse's hoofs making no noise, it was not till he got in front of the hut that the dog, ever found as its guardian (either well-bred deer-hound or cur of low degree), came bounding up towards him, barking loudly. In this case the animal was a remarkably handsome deer-hound, of a size and strength sufficient to drag him from his horse. The hut-keeper was seated in a rough sort of easy-chair, and was apparently fast asleep.

"Hillo, my man, call off your dog, or he and I may do each other an injury," shouted Arthur; "he is a noble brute, and I should not like to hurt him, if I could help it!"

The man started up, a book dropping from his hand. "Come back, good Brian; come back, sir!" he cried out. "I must apologise, Mr Gilpin, for not hearing you; but I was overcome, I believe, by the heat," he added, as he took the horse from which Arthur had just dismounted.

As the stock-keeper unsaddled the animal, Arthur's eye fell on the open page of the book from which he had been reading. It was a superior edition of Horace, well used.

Roughly clad and unshorn and haggard in his looks as the man was, Arthur could not but conclude that he had once moved among the educated classes of society. The ever-ready damper and pot of tea were produced; and Arthur, having satisfied his appetite, made the usual inquiries about the station. Everything seemed to be satisfactory.

"You appear to be fond of reading," said Arthur, glancing at the Horace, which had been placed on a shelf among a few other books.

"Ah! a friend of my early days. He serves to beguile many a weary hour," answered the hut-keeper, with a sigh.

Arthur did not like to ask questions. "We brought a few books with us into the bush; I shall be glad to lend them to you," he said.

"They will be most acceptable, sir," said the hut-keeper, his countenance brightening; "my own stock is small, and I have read each volume over and over again till I know them by heart. I believe that if a chest of new books were to reach me, like the half-starved wretch who suddenly finds himself in the midst of plenty, I could sit down and read till my eyesight or my wits had left me."

"I can enter into your feelings," said Arthur kindly. "The life you lead must indeed be dull."

"Ah! it might be far worse, though," answered the hut-keeper; "poverty out here can scarcely be said to pinch. I often ask myself what might it have been, or what certainly would it have been, had I remained in London till my last shilling was gone. To rot in a poorhouse or to sweep a crossing would have been my lot, or there might have been a worse alternative. I had enough left to pay my passage out here. It was a wise move—the only wise thing I ever did in my life. My expectations on landing were foolish, and before I could realise them I had the chance of going to gaol or becoming a hut-keeper." The last remarks were made as he stood holding the rein of Arthur's horse.

Arthur rode round the run, inspected the flock, and had to pass near the hut again on his return homeward. The hut-keeper, Charles Craven he called himself, was on the watch for him.

"I must have a word with you, Mr Gilpin," he said. "You are the first man I have met since I landed on these shores who has sympathised with me. I would do something to serve you. First, I must warn you never to be unarmed, either in your hut or out of it; and especially advise you and your brother, when you ride out, always to keep together. Many of the hands on the station are exasperated with you for your style of proceeding, and they think that if they could get rid of you they would have things their own way."

Thanking Craven for his advice, Arthur pushed on towards home as rapidly as his grey would carry him. He was relieved on finding that James had just before arrived. He told his brother of the warning Craven had given him.

James was at first inclined to laugh at it. "The scoundrels dare not injure us!" he exclaimed. Then he remembered Basham's revengeful looks, and the surly manner of several of the hands, and finally agreed with his brother that it would be wiser to go armed, and keep together.

They had removed the hut-keeper to another post, and placed Green in charge of their abode. This would have been necessary, if for no other reason, for the purpose of having it kept clean and habitable, which the dirty habits of the former occupant rendered impracticable. The exact situation of the hut has not been described. It stood on a hillside, the ground immediately round it cleared, but with bush both above it and on either side, extending to a considerable distance. In some places the trees were fine and lofty, in others only stringy-bark or low bushes. A river passed in front at the distance of less than a quarter of a mile, full and flowing in winter, but after the heats of summer consisting of a succession of water-holes connected by a trickling rill. During the shearing season the river was a scene of the greatest animation, as all the flocks from far and near were driven up to it, that the sheep might be washed before being deprived of their fleeces. After a sudden downfall of rain, the quiet stream became a roaring, boiling torrent, sweeping onward with terrific force, now forming a wide lake, and, once more confined by high and narrow banks, whirling along with rapid eddies; and at spots, where a few hours before a person could pass on foot, the current would test the strength of the strongest swimmer or most powerful horse to cross; at other times it relapsed into a state of silence, not without much picturesque beauty of a tranquil character. The hut commanded a view of the river, but it, as well as the sheds, sheep-folds, and stock-yards, were placed far too high above it to be reached by the widest inundation it could cause.

Arthur did not forget his promise to Craven, and, as soon as he was able, he rode toward his hut with several books in his pockets. The hut-keeper was very grateful, and expressed himself in a way which showed that he was really a gentleman and a man of feeling. The brothers, as they rode away, agreed that it would be but an act of common kindness to ask him to visit them, and that they might send another man to take his place.

Craven considered a moment. "No; I had better not," he answered; "the men about here look upon me as one of themselves, and if I were seen with you, I should no longer be trusted by them. They are mischievously inclined; and if I can turn them from their purposes, or give you warning of their intentions, and help, if needs be, it will afford me the satisfaction of believing that I have been of some little use in

W. H. G. Kingston

the world."

They could not but agree with him, and expressed a hope that an employment more suited to a person of his education might be found for him.

Craven gave a sickly smile. "You are young, and think change is easy," he said. "The sapling is quickly bent, but when an old tree has long grown in the same direction, it cannot be straightened again. Supply me with books and tobacco, and, a few years hence, perhaps, a pair of spectacles, and I shall have no desire to quit these wilds."

"Perhaps you will change your mind," said James, putting out his hand, which the broken-down gentleman shook warmly.

Many years had passed since his palm had pressed that of an equal in intellect and education. It seemed to raise him out of the state of hopeless apathy into which he had fallen.

The hut at headquarters had greatly improved in appearance since it had become the residence of the Gilpins. There were three glazed windows, and it was partitioned off into a bedroom, a sitting-room—where books and papers could be arranged on shelves and kept clean—and a kitchen, which served as dining-room and hall. A good-sized storeroom had been built at the back, with a door opening into the kitchen. They and Sam Green were the only inmates of the building.

It was late at night, the Bible had been read, and family prayers had been offered up—when two or three were gathered together that custom was never departed from in that rude hut in the wilds of Australia—thanksgivings for past, petitions for future protection. Sam had thrown himself on his bed in a corner of the hall, and his loud snoring told that he was fast asleep. The brothers had been reading in their sitting-room, and were on the point of retiring to bed, when a slight tap was heard at the window. They thought it was some night bird attracted by the light, and took no notice. A louder tap was heard; Arthur opened the window.

"Wisht! mister, dear; just let me in, for I've something to say to ye," said a voice, which he recognised to be Larry Killock's.

"I will let you in by the door, Larry, unless you like to jump through the window," said Arthur.

"The quickest way's the best," was the answer, as Larry leaped through the opening, adding, "shut the shutters, lest any one's eyes should be looking this way." Larry was out of breath, and looked faint and weary, as if he had come a long distance.

"What brings you here, Larry?" said Arthur, in a tone of anxiety, which it was natural he should feel.

"It's bad news I've to tell yer honours; but if I'd had to lose my life, I'd have come to tell it," he answered. "No matter how I found it out, but I did find it out, that the people on the station, just because you have put a stop to their robberies and rogueries, have determined to do away with you. As villains is mostly cowards, there's none of them dares to bell the cat themselves, and so they've engaged some of them black fellows—the thieves of the world—to do the job for them. It was to be done quickly, and I came along, ignorant entirely if I'd be in time or not to save yer honours' lives; but they've not killed you yet, and we'll see if we can't be a match for them." The Irishman went on to say that the plan proposed was to set fire to the surrounding bush, and that while they ran out, as they naturally would, to stop the

W. H. G. Kingston

flames from approaching their dwelling, by cutting down the surrounding grass and bushes, they were to be knocked down with boomerangs by the blacks, and their bodies dragged into the fire.

The brothers immediately decided what to do. Waking up Sam and telling him what they had heard, they bade Larry take care of the house and make a good supper; and, reaping-hooks and axes in hand, they sailed out to clear the ground of all fuel capable of bringing the flames up to the hut. Beginning at the back of the building, they worked away energetically, gradually extending their circle till they had cut down and raked away all fuel, almost up to the woods, when they heard Sam's voice calling them—

"Come back, come back! the black fellows are close upon us! I wasn't comfortable in my mind, and went out to listen. I heard them calling to each other, and their dogs barking."

Although they believed that the bullock-driver's anxiety or fears might somewhat exaggerate the danger, they felt that it was, at all events, prudent to retreat to their hut. All remained quiet: they were beginning to hope that the alarm might be a false one. Arthur again went out, and as, rifle in hand, he was pacing as sentry round the hut, he saw a bright light burst forth above the trees, half a mile or so off to the south-west. He watched it for some minutes; it increased, extending on either hand, the forked points of the flames appearing high above the intervening trees. There could be no doubt that the wood was on fire. Thus far the information obtained by the bullock-driver was correct. There was too much reason, therefore, to fear that their destruction would be attempted by the savages. He hurried into the hut to consult what was best to be done. Their horses were at hand; they might mount them and ride away from the danger; but such a proceeding was not to be thought of. If, however, they were not secured, they would be carried off by the blacks. Arthur and Sam accordingly went out and brought them up to the hut; there was just room for them to stand in the kitchen by removing the table; the door was then closed and barred. None of the party, however, felt inclined to wait inactive till the conflagration reached their neighbourhood without knowing what progress it was making. There was no window at the back of the hut.

"We will make holes in the roof," said Arthur; "we shall be able to see through them what is going on, and if we are besieged in our fortress by the savages, we shall be the better able to defend ourselves and annoy them."

A stool, placed on the top of the table, enabled them to reach the roof, and by stringing some boards to the rafters, they found convenient standing places. The square holes cut in the shingles forming the roof gave them a look-out. There was enough in the spectacle they beheld to try the courage of the stoutest hearted. In front of them, that is to say, at the back of the hut, was a narrow neck of forest, which was as yet intact, but above the branches—between the stems which stood out in bold relief—the flames were seen raging furiously, devouring, as they advanced, everything in their course, both to the right and to the left. Strange sounds, too, were heard: there was the roaring, hissing, and crackling of the fire, and ever and anon a report like that of heavy guns, as some tall tree was riven in two by the intense heat which surrounded it; the air also came like a blast from a furnace, laden with smoke, ashes, and often sparks, which threatened to ignite the dry roof of the building. The danger was increasing, for the flames were advancing towards the confines of the wood nearest them. Now the fire, snake-like, would be seen creeping along the grass, then catching hold of some bush, which would speedily be wrapped in its deadly embrace; next the lower boughs of the trees would

W. H. G. Kingston

catch, or the dry wood and twigs round the stumps, and upward it would mount triumphant, roaring and crackling— the slighter trees falling prostrate before it; the older and thicker still withstanding its fierce assault, though left branchless and blackened, with all vitality destroyed.

As yet the hut remained uninjured, though a semicircle of fire raged furiously close to it, and here and there, where a bush still stood, or some tufts of grass had not been closely cropped, the flames made advances, and, winding along the ground, rose up, flickered, and died. From the first outbreak of the conflagration various animals had been seen crossing the open ground, as they escaped from the burning forest. Birds innumerable, of varied plumage, aroused from their roosting places, flew by, some uttering discordant screams of terror, many, with scorched wings, falling dead before they reached the hut. As yet no human beings had been seen.

"I trust that the savages will not venture to attack us," said James; "only in the last extremity could I feel justified in firing at them."

"Arrah! it's but little of that sort of treatment they have received since the white man first put his foot on their shores," observed Larry. "I've heard tell of their being shot down by scores at a time, like vermin. Many and many's the black fellow I've seen killed, and no notice taken of it, and no thought by the man who did the deed, any more than if he had fired at a wild beast."

Arthur interrupted Larry's remarks by exclaiming, "There they are, though, and in no small numbers too, just coming round the edge of the burning wood to the south-east!"

The rest of the party looked in the direction indicated, and there, seen clearly by the light of the flames thrown on their dark bodies, armed with spears, clubs, and boomerangs, was a numerous body of savages. They appeared to be looking cautiously about, as if expecting to find their intended victims engaged in extinguishing the flames round the hut.

"The black chaps are no cowards, Mr Gilpin. We shall have a fierce fight of it, and our three firearms won't do much against all them, I'm thinking," observed Larry.

"There are still more of them coming!" exclaimed Arthur; "and see! there's a fellow has just joined them who looks like a chief. They are pointing this way. We may look out to be attacked in a few minutes. We may fire surely, James, if they come on? A few shots will probably send them scampering off. They have no firearms among them."

"Not so sure of that, yer honour," said Larry. "Look, the fellow you called the chief has a gun of some sort, and he is showing it to the rest to encourage them. He handles it like a man who knows the use of it, too."

In spite of the overwhelming numbers of the enemy, the little garrison resolved to maintain their position. Little could be gained by flight, and all their property would inevitably be destroyed should they desert the hut. The risk they ran in either case was very great. They might pick off some of the savages, but there were so many that they might easily surround the hut and burn it to the ground.

"If we had two or three more fellows with us, we might bid defiance to the whole mob," said Arthur.

"To my mind, if we was to shoot down that chap with the gun in his hand, the rest would show us their heels," observed Sam Green, who had not before spoken since the appearance of the savages; "they none on 'em shows much

W. H. G. Kingston

stomach for the fight."

Sam's remark was correct. The savages were evidently aware that the defenders of the hut possessed firearms, and even the chief showed no inclination to expose himself. From their movements, however, it appeared that they were about to make a rush towards the hut. At that instant the tramp of horses' hoofs was heard approaching, and a voice cried out—

"Open the door! Be quick! Let us in!"

James and his brother, who had been watching the savages from the roof, jumped down at the moment that a rifle-ball whistled by.

"That bullet was never fired by a black chap," said Larry to Sam, as they also descended from their perches to receive the new-comers. The Gilpins, without hesitation, opened the door, and Craven with a stranger appeared, just dismounting from their horses, whose foam-covered bits and reeking backs showed that they had ridden at no slow rate.

"No time for words. If you have room for our poor brutes, take them in; if not, they must run their chance outside," he said. "Here, we have brought arms and ammunition. We knew that you would be hard pressed, and have come to share your fate."

"Come in, come in," said James, leading in the horses, who, trembling with fatigue, were quiet enough.

The new-comers had brought a rifle, a musket, and two fowling-pieces, with powder-flasks and bullets. This reinforcement raised the confidence of the little party in the hut. The blacks, discovering Craven and his companion, made a rush to intercept them. They sprang in after the horses; but before the door was closed, a shower of darts and boomerangs rattled against it, and again a shot was heard, and a bullet flew by among them. Those inside hurriedly closed the door; but, almost before the bar could be replaced, the blacks were thundering with their clubs against it. James had been strongly averse to shed blood, even the blood of savages endeavouring to destroy him and his companions, yet there was no longer any other alternative; the blacks must be driven off, or they would burn down the hut. It became James's duty to take the command, and to give the word. Loop-holes were speedily cut in the walls.

"Be ready, friends; pick off the leaders, each of us those more immediately in front as we stand. Do not throw a shot away. Fire!"

Three of the blacks were seen to fall to the ground, the rest ran back in disorder, two of them wounded. This gave the defenders of the hut time to reload and to make some fresh loop-holes. The blacks were again met by the chief, who was seen urging them to return, though he showed no inclination to place himself in danger. Craven, seeing the look-out places in the roof, proposed getting up there.

"I think that I might bring down that fellow if I could get a steady shot at him," he said, taking up his rifle. "The fellow has disappeared!" he exclaimed. "I cannot make it out, yet the rest obey him, for they are coming on again, and with fire-brands, too. We must beat them, or they will roast us."

The spectacle was indeed appalling. There were from fifty to sixty blacks, each with a burning brand in his left hand and a spear or club in the other, all leaping and shrieking in concert, as they sprang on towards the hut. The defenders waited till they got within thirty paces, and then all together fired. The result was the same as before. Several fell, others

W. H. G. Kingston

ran howling back wounded, the rest, throwing down their brands, followed. Another volley was sent after them, in the hope that it might induce them to abandon the attack. Craven reloaded, and sat watching at his post. The crack of his rifle was again heard.

"I have hit the scoundrel!" he exclaimed. "He is no black man; he is ordering them to lift him up; they are carrying him off. I have not the heart to send another bullet through him, but he deserves it."

"We may capture him, though," cried Arthur. "Let us jump on our horses; we shall soon overtake them."

The proposal was instantly adopted; no one was more eager and full of animation than Craven. The horses were led out, and, Larry remaining with the spare firearms in the hut, the party urged on the animals in the direction the blacks had gone. The flames of the burning forest lighted up the country, and enabled them to ride at full speed, though it was with difficulty they could make the horses keep near the fire, edging along which the blacks had gone, hoping probably, if they could get round the furthest end, to place it between themselves and those they had so ruthlessly attacked. Mounting to the top of a ridge, the horsemen caught sight of a party of natives on a hill before them, with a valley intervening. The blacks got to the top, on some open ground, when it was seen that they were carrying a burden among them. The white men dashed down into the valley, and, making their way across it, urged their horses up the opposite height. The blacks saw them coming; in vain the man they were carrying ordered them to remain by him. Oaths, entreaties, promises were of no avail. Putting him down, they ran off as fast as their legs would carry them.

The last exclamations he uttered showed his pursuers that he was no native. They were in English, and too horrible to be repeated. The Gilpins reached him. He glared fiercely at them as they dismounted, and seemed to be feeling for a pistol in his belt. They grasped his hands to prevent his using it. The oath he uttered betrayed him. Though his face and arms and the upper part of his body was blackened, they at once recognised him as Basham, the late overseer. The wretched blacks had already suffered so severely that the settlers had no desire to overtake them. Dismounting, therefore, one of the party led the horses, and the rest, lifting up the wounded man, bore him back towards the hut. They frequently looked behind to ascertain if the blacks were following for the purpose of recovering him, but no attempt of the sort was made. It was hard work carrying him, for he was a heavy man. Some deep groans which burst from him showed that he was suffering much pain. From a feeling of mercy they stopped, and found that the bullet had entered his leg, and had probably grazed, if it had not broken, the bone. Craven had a knowledge of surgery, especially valuable to a bushman; and while all were stooping down round the injured man, he probed the wound, and extracted some of the black cloth which had been carried into it. Had Basham been a friend who had been fighting for them, he could not have been treated more tenderly. He, however, scarcely spoke, and displayed no sign of gratitude. At length they reached the hut in safety. The horses were tethered outside, ready for instant service. The wounded man was placed on Sam's bed, and such restoratives as the brothers possessed administered to him. These arrangements concluded, the whole party thankfully sat down to a meal, which was rather breakfast than supper. The Gilpins now learned from Craven that he had heard a rumour of the proposed attack of the savages, instigated by the stockmen, though he did not understand that Basham was the prime mover; that there was only one man whom he could trust, and that, having invited him, they had both set forward to their assistance. His companion was evidently, like himself, a man of superior education and fallen fortunes. In Craven the necessity for unusual exertion had worked a marked change, and he no longer appeared the spirit-broken man he had seemed when Arthur first met him.

The fire continued raging, but made no further progress, and, in spite of its dangerous neighbourhood, all the party except James, who insisted on remaining on watch, were fast asleep. The hours of darkness passed by slowly and anxiously. He kept his ears ever ready to catch any sound outside, and he occasionally looked forth, thinking it possible that the blacks might return, or that some of the white companions of their prisoner might come to look for him. The nearest police-station was about thirty miles off. It was necessary to convey their prisoner there; but then it was very possible that they might be attacked on the road, and that he might be rescued. Knowing the bad feeling of the people around them, it would be imprudent to weaken the strength of their party at the hut. James therefore resolved, if Larry was sufficiently rested, to send him off, as soon as it was daylight, for a sufficient force to escort the late overseer to prison. Scarcely had he formed this plan when Larry jumped up, and exclaimed—

"Now, yer honour, you have had watching enough, and I'll just take my spell. I'm as fresh as a daisy with the dew on the grass."

James declined doing this, and told him of his proposed plan.

"Nothing like taking time by the forelock!" exclaimed the Irishman. "I've my raisons, and I'll be off—as soon as I can stow some food in my inside and catch the horse—before it is daylight, so that it will be a hard job for any of them fellows to find me, even if they have a fancy for that same."

As there was no time to be lost, James went out and brought

in Larry's horse, to which he gave a sop of damper and spirits and water, while Larry was refreshing himself.

"It's good luck I'll have on a good errand, I hope," he exclaimed, as he leaped into the saddle; "for though the police and I weren't over friendly once on a time, I can now face them like an honest man, thanks to yer honour."

Larry was soon lost to sight in the gloom which prevailed at a distance from the yet burning wood. Daylight came. All hands were on foot. The wounded man appeared to be no worse. A sad change had taken place in the once picturesque appearance of the surrounding scenery. In the place of the green wood, with many noble trees, a few blackened stems, gaunt and branchless, with still smouldering ashes at their base, were the only objects to be seen on the hillside. The Gilpins scarcely liked to keep Craven and his companion from their posts, though at the same time they felt the importance of having a sufficient guard over their prisoner. They were surprised that none of the stockmen or hut-keepers from the neighbourhood had made their appearance. It proved but too plainly that all were disaffected; and it made them resolve not to quit the vicinity of the hut till the arrival of the police. They could not, however, come for some hours. Breakfast was just over, when Green, who had gone down to fetch some water from the river, came hurrying back, and reported that he had seen several men collecting, with arms in their hands, on the opposite side. "Who could they be? What could be their object?" was the question.

It was decided that while every precaution should be taken to prevent surprise, they should be treated as if they could only have come on a friendly errand, and that every attempt should be made to conciliate them before resorting to force. Scarcely five minutes had passed before several men were seen approaching, from the direction of the river, in single file. They were all disguised, either with blackened faces or masks, while they wore either kangaroo or sheep skins over their shoulders, or were covered with the thick-leaved branches of shrubs, so as completely to conceal their figures. It was evident that they intended mischief. They halted at about twenty paces from the hut, seemingly surprised at finding the windows barricaded and the door closed, with the muzzles of firearms protruding from the walls. Seeing their hesitation, James instantly went out, and, with his rifle in his hand, confronted them—

"Men, you have amused yourselves seemingly with what might be a harmless mummery, were it not for the weapons in your hands," he began, in a firm tone; "put them down, and let me hear what you have got to say."

The leading man, after consulting with his companions, replied, "You have got shut up there a friend of ours, and you must give him up to us, or take the consequences."

"I am not at all likely to yield to demands made by strangers in the tone you make them, or to tell you whether or not we have any one shut up inside this hut," said James; "you will risk your own lives, and gain nothing by persisting in such folly."

"Yours is the folly, master, in refusing our demands!" exclaimed the man. "You can gain no good by keeping the man a prisoner, but will do him and us harm!"

While the man was speaking, he and his companions advanced still closer to the hut.

"Stand back!" cried James, endeavouring to bring his piece to his shoulder; but before he had done so, the men, stooping low, sprang forward, keeping him between themselves and the hut. Those inside opened the door to admit him, but instead of retreating he stood fast, till the leader of the ruffians had struck up his rifle, and, grasping him by the throat, bore him backwards. Arthur, rushing out to his rescue, was seized likewise, and the whole party dashed together into the hut, overthrowing Green, who came out to help his young masters. Fortunately their eyes first fell on the wounded man as he lay on a bed in the outer room. The stretcher of boughs, on which he had been brought to the hut, still remained outside. A few words passed between them. They lifted him on the litter, neither the Gilpins nor Green being able to prevent them, and, with a shout of triumph, they carried him off towards the river. The Gilpins and Green were quickly on their feet. For an instant they stood irresolute whether to follow.

"Do not attempt it," cried a voice from within; "the villains will not scruple to fire if you do."

It was Craven who spoke. James was inclined to accuse him of cowardice till he reflected at what risk he had come voluntarily to their assistance. Craven himself, too, explained that being assured the outlaws would murder him and his companion had they seen them, they had retreated into the storeroom, where they lay hid among casks and cases. It was provoking to have lost their prisoner, but at the same time they had reason to be thankful that no life had been sacrificed.

"If they find out from Basham that we are here, they will to a certainty return," observed Craven; "and we must be prepared."

"The police will be here by that time," was Arthur's remark. "If they come, we may follow, and we should have our horses ready."

"None of them said a word about the police," observed James; "I don't think that they were aware that we expected them."

"Then, depend on it, when they find out that Richards and I are away from our posts, they will return to punish us. Basham will not say anything, however, till he thinks that they have placed him in safety, and then, of course, he will tell them of our being here."

In consequence of Craven's very just apprehensions, the party set to work to fortify the hut more completely, by putting stronger bars to the windows and doors, and by placing a stockade outside at the weaker parts, so as to make it more difficult for any assailants to reach the roof.

These preparations were scarcely completed, when Green, who happened to be on the roof, cried out—

"There come the chaps again, and twice as many as before!"

This was serious news; for it was not likely that the ruffian band would have returned, unless with the intention of destroying those who had offended them. It is very probable that they hoped to make it appear that the blacks, having set the wood on fire, had afterwards killed them. The whole party in the hut felt, therefore, that they must fight to the last extremity. A line was drawn round the building, and it was agreed that if an enemy passed it they would fire; but they would refrain as long as possible from shedding blood. They had scarcely time to barricade the door and windows before the outlaws appeared, mounting the hill from the river, not as before, in single file, but scattered over the ground, so as to take advantage of the shelter any inequalities might afford.

Some were disguised, but there were several blacks who were in their usual unclothed state, and were evidently not masqueraders. It might have been difficult to identify even those, as their faces and bodies were bedaubed with pigments in strange and hideous devices.

This time James took care not to show himself. "Stand back, men!" he shouted in a loud voice. "If any one advances across the line we have marked out, we must fire. We do not wish to shed blood, but the consequence be on your own heads. Back, black men! you get killed."

The outlaws hesitated, and even the natives seemed to understand what was said. Whereabouts the magic line was drawn, at which some of them would be certain to lose their lives, they could not tell. Soldiers in battle will dare any danger, but villains engaged in a criminal act are always cowards, unless driven to desperation. Such was not the case at present. A white handkerchief was shown on a stick, and a voice cried out—

"We don't want to hurt you, Mr Gilpin, or your brother, or man, but there are two fellows there, and we must have them; give them up to us, and we will go away."

"I ask you, would you give up people who had put confidence in you?" said James.

"We have nothing to say to that; give up the men, or we will burn down the hut and you in it," was the answer.

"Remember the warning I have given you," said James; "however, we will just talk the matter over, and let you know what we decide."

"Be sharp about it, then," said the first speaker; "we did not come here to shilly-shally, and we shall advance directly the time is up. We give you five minutes to settle the matter."

"We must take ten; and recollect that our rifles will be kept ready for use," added James, firmly.

"I am afraid the fellows will put their threat into execution," said Craven. "Now, you see, our lives are of no use to any one, and so, when the ten minutes are up, tell them that we will go with them, if they will take their departure quietly, and not injure you."

"On no account would we do so!" exclaimed the brothers in the same breath. "I would not trust them, even if we should be base enough to give you up."

"Noa, sur; I'd sooner cut out my tongue than give ye up to them arrant knaves!" exclaimed Green, doubling his fist, and shaking it in the direction he supposed that the outlaws were collected.

The minutes passed slowly by. They were doubtful whether the outlaws would begin the attack at the end of the five minutes, or wait till the termination of the ten. The dread of the fatal line, however, seemed to keep them back. The muzzles of the firearms were kept protruding from the walls, and, as there were several pistols as well as rifles, they made a good display of force, rather damping the courage of those who came expecting, probably, an easy victory.

The ten minutes came to an end, and fully another five had passed by, and the outlaws did not advance. It was very clear, therefore, that they had not intercepted Larry, nor were aware that he had gone for the police. How long it might be before they could arrive it was impossible to say; perhaps when Larry reached their quarters the larger number had been sent in an opposite direction, and considerable time might be lost. However, the importance of gaining as much time as possible was very great; for though the little garrison did not despair of beating off the enemy, they earnestly desired to avoid the bloodshed which must ensue if fighting once began.

James therefore waited with a sad and beating heart to give the fatal order, should the outlaws overstep the prescribed boundary.

"Well, what are you going to do?" shouted one of the men; "are you going to give up those fellows?"

"Who is it you are looking for?" asked James, glad of any means to spin out the time.

"Gentleman Jim and Sulking Sam," was the answer. "Come, turn them out; you've got them."

"I know no men by those names," said James.

"The rogues are right enough, though. I have the honour of being designated as 'Gentleman Jim,'" said Craven, with a smile.

"I say, what are the right names of the chaps?" asked one of the outlaws of a comrade.

"I never knowed 'em by any other," was the answer.

"Come, come, master, you hand them out, and be done with it!" cried several of the men together.

"Supposing they were with us, and that we were to deliver them into your hands, what would you do with them?"

asked James.

"Hang them up on the nearest tree, as we will you also, if you don't come to terms pretty quickly!" shouted the first ruffian who had spoken.

"I won't help you to be guilty of so great a crime," said James; "think better of it, and go away."

"No more of this; time's up!" cried a loud voice. "Charge, lads!"

The whole body sprang forward towards the hut. The whites instantly began firing their muskets or fowling-pieces, the blacks at the same moment casting their spears.

"Hurra! Here come the police! Look out for yourselves!" cried Sam Green, who had been keeping watch at a hole near the roof, looking eastward.

The words, uttered before any one had time to reload, had a magic effect. One of the outlaws, springing on one side to ascertain whether the announcement was true, shouted out the fact to his comrades. Down the hill they rushed, as fast as their legs could carry them. Their bullets had either passed over the hut or had lodged in the thick planking which formed the sides, without injuring any of those within. The sound of the shots, however, made the police put spurs to their horses' sides, and they came galloping up as the last of the outlaws disappeared across the river. Their steeds were pretty well knocked up with their long and rapid journey, but Lieutenant Graham, the officer in command, was most anxious to catch some of the men. "We will join you!" cried Craven, running out. Their horses were found in a grassy nook to the left. Craven, with his friend Richards, and Arthur Gilpin, and ten of the police, led by their officer, joined in the pursuit. Before long they came in sight of the outlaws, scattered far and wide over the country, each man endeavouring to make his escape by himself. Most of them had thrown away the boughs and the skins with which they had been covered. Three men kept closer together than did the rest. Craven, who thought he recognised them by their figures as stockmen belonging to the station, recommended that they should be followed. The men soon discovered that they especially were pursued. When they saw that all chance of escape was gone, they turned round and stood at bay; but as the troopers advanced with drawn sabres, they threw down their arms and cried out for quarter. Their lives were of course spared, but their hands being lashed behind them, they were conducted back to the hut. Another man was caught, but the rest were allowed to escape. "We can always get any we require," observed one of the police. The prisoners were the men Craven supposed. He himself was the chief cause of their being taken. Except that his dress was rough, as usual, his whole manner was changed as he galloped across the field. Graham looked at him more than once with astonishment.

They were all once more collected in the hut, doing justice to the fare Sam and Larry had provided.

"I am nearly certain that I know you!" said the police officer, addressing Craven. "My name is Graham, and yours is—"

"All right, old fellow!" cried Craven, jumping up and grasping his hand; "it is pleasant, indeed, to meet a near relation out here. I never heard of your coming."

"Nor did I know of your being here. However, we will not lose sight of each other again," said the lieutenant.

As scarcely any of the stockmen or hut-keepers could be

W. H. G. Kingston

trusted, the Gilpins begged that some of the police might remain, while they went round to drive in and concentrate the herds of cattle and the flocks of sheep, now probably without keepers, and subject to the depredations of the outlaws. It was very hard work; but, with the help of Craven, a few of the better-disposed men, who were found at their huts (having probably returned there after the ill-success of their expedition), were selected, and the task was accomplished. Fresh hands were sent for. Craven was appointed overseer, with his friend under him. Graham set off with his prisoners for headquarters, Norfolk Island being, without doubt, their ultimate destination. No tidings could be gained of Basham. He was probably hid away in the mountains, but it was not likely that he would make any further attempts on the station. The disorderly servants were dismissed, fresh ones arrived, and for some time the affairs entrusted to the young settlers went on quietly and prosperously.

CHAPTER FIVE

The Gilpins found Craven a great addition to their social circle in their remote station. They, more than ever, required support and assistance, for depressing news began to reach them from Sydney. The financial affairs of the colony had for some time past been in an unsatisfactory state. Money for paying the men was often considerably in arrear; and stores and provisions were sent up only in small quantities and of an inferior quality. At length, a letter arrived from the agent, directing them to send produce to Sydney, to meet certain heavy liabilities. As wool was not forthcoming, they were to boil down both cattle and sheep, to dismiss a large number of the men, and to practise the most rigid economy. The requisite boilers and casks for the tallow soon afterwards arrived. It was most disagreeable and painful work. Flock after flock of sheep were driven in and slaughtered; the carcases were put into the cauldrons, the fat was packed in the casks, and the hides roughly dried; while the meat, which might have fed thousands of the starving poor in the old country, was allowed, of necessity, to rot uselessly on the ground. Theirs was no solitary instance of the consequence of want of capital to carry on business, for such was the condition to which the greater number of squatters throughout the colony were reduced. Fortunately, tallow and hides were in demand, and realised high prices, and thus many of the settlers were soon able to get out of their difficulties, though left with sadly diminished flocks and herds. The Gilpins and their overseer, Craven, spared no exertion to save, as far as possible, the loss of property. One day Arthur had gone in search of some cattle, which had strayed among the range of mountains to the west. After looking for them in vain, he was returning, annoyed and out of spirits, when he observed a stream issuing from the side of a hill, with the banks on either side encrusted with a glittering white substance. He tasted it, and found it perfectly salt. Collecting a pocketful, he returned home with his spirits completely revived. All the party were of opinion that it was a salt spring; that others would be found in the neighbourhood; and that salt could be manufactured with which the meat, which was now lost, might be preserved either for sale or for future consumption. The next morning they eagerly set out for the spot. They were not disappointed. Other springs were found. By evaporation alone, a small supply could be procured; and with some simple apparatus they hoped to produce as much as they would require. A cauldron and some pans were sent up, and after a few experiments they succeeded to their satisfaction; and they were able to send into Sydney, with the next dray-load of tallow, a cask of salted hams and tongues.

About this time, they received a letter from their first friend in the colony, Mr Prentiss, saying that the losses of his family had been so great, and that his father had so taken it to heart, that he was completely prostrate, and not likely to survive. He had, therefore, himself come up to take the management of affairs, accompanied by his children. He requested James to come and pay him a visit without delay. Leaving Arthur and Craven in charge, he at once set off. He rode alone, though he would probably have to camp out one or two nights. There were stations on the road, but they were at inconvenient distances; and unless compelled by bad weather, he did not purpose stopping at them. He had a gun as a protection; but he had no fear of bushrangers. They were now seldom heard of in the colony. From wild beasts to be dreaded by a traveller, Australia is, happily, free. He was not likely to meet any blacks inclined to be unfriendly. Occasionally the natives murdered hut-keepers and stock-men, but in most instances they had been provoked to do so by ill-treatment. With saddle-bags and holsters well filled, a blanket, a tin kettle and pot, strapped to the saddle before him, he set forth on his journey. There is an elasticity in the atmosphere and a freedom from restraint which makes travelling on horseback in Australia most delightful. James Gilpin enjoyed it to the full. He also found it good to be alone occasionally, to commune with his heart; and this journey gave him ample opportunity of being so. The first day passed over pleasantly. He had arranged to spend the evening with an acquaintance on the road. As his own shadow and that of his steed were lengthened out on the grass, the smoke of his friend's hut, curling up among the gum trees, appeared before him. He called out as he rode up to the door, but no voice answered; the distant sound, however, of tinkling sheep bells told him that the flock of the station was being driven into a pen for the night, where the new-born lambs could be better protected from the dingoes and hawks, their chief enemies, than if left on the open. Unsaddling and turning his horse into a paddock near at hand, he entered the hut. The kettle was hissing on the fire, and the damper was baking under it. There were signs that the hut was the residence of a gentleman (though all was in the rough), and evidently that of a bachelor. Every spot on the walls was covered with shooting and fishing gear, sporting prints, and some of a better description; and there was a book-case, with thoroughly used volumes, and coats and hats hung up, and shelves loaded with all sorts of articles, and chests below, and casks, one with flour ready open; the corners also were crowded. There was a bed-chamber boarded off for the owner, a refinement not very often indulged in, and a bunk at one end of the general room, for the hut-keeper. The cheery voice of the proprietor addressing his dogs announced his return. He warmly greeted his neighbour (their abodes were only forty miles apart); and tea, damper, cold beef, and pork were speedily on the table.

The two settlers were merry and contented, in spite of misfortunes. Johnstone had also been compelled to boil down.

"Now is the time for a fellow with five or six hundred pounds to lay the foundation of a fortune," he observed; "both cattle and sheep can be bought at a mere nominal price. I must sell or boil down still more of mine; but I see my way clearly out of my difficulties, and keep up my spirits."

The hint was not lost upon James. He had been unwilling to take any of his employers' cattle, lest it might throw him open to suspicion; but he now resolved to offer to purchase some, and, at all events, to take all that Mr Johnstone might wish to sell. Local subjects were of course discussed.

"By-the-by," observed Mr Johnstone, "we were surprised some days ago at seeing a white man lurking about here, dressed in skins and rags. The people thought he must be mad; for whenever they approached him, he ran off howling into the bush. I ordered some food to be placed for him at a spot where we could watch him. He saw us, and would not approach; but after watching for some time we went away, and he then must have darted out from his concealment and carried off the food, for when we returned it was gone. From that day he disappeared, and whether he has been drowned in some river or water-hole, or has been starved in the bush, I cannot say."

James Gilpin started at an early hour the next morning, intending to make a long day's journey, and to camp out, as he must in that case do. His horse, a peculiarly fine and strong one, bore him well through the early part of the day. In the afternoon he entered a forest, extending on either side to a considerable distance. The track through it was less defined than usual, still, by constant reference to his compass, when he had any doubts, he had no fear about making a mistake.

He had ridden on for some distance, when he observed that the sky was overcast, and the wind began to moan among the trees. Suddenly, with a spring which would have thrown a worse rider, his horse started at a vivid flash of lightning which darted from the sky, struck a huge tree near him, tearing off a large limb, and then ran hissing along the ground. A crash of thunder, such as he had really heard, followed, and he found it impossible to prevent his affrighted steed from setting off at full gallop among the trees. It was with the greatest difficulty that he could guide the animal, so as to save his legs from being dashed against the trunks and his head against the branches. Crash succeeded crash in rapid succession, and at times so vivid was the lightning that the forest seemed one blaze of fire. In vain he searched for an open space where he might, at all events, be free from the danger of being crushed by falling branches. Now he thought he saw an opening on one side, now on the other; but each time he was disappointed. He discovered, however, that he had got out of the track, and when he began to consider in which direction he should go, he was under the somewhat painful feeling that he had lost his way. He put his hand in his pocket to examine his compass; it was not there. Again and again he searched for it; nowhere was it to be found. It had undoubtedly been jerked out of his pocket during some of the violent springs his steed had made when frightened by the lightning. He had not the remotest hope of finding it on

W. H. G. Kingston

the ground, and would therefore not waste time in looking for it. Just as he had made this disagreeable discovery, the fury of the storm abated, and he was in hopes that it was about to cease altogether. He rode forward, he believed, towards the east. If he could get out of the wood he might still reach a station before dark, considerably short of the distance he hoped to have made good that day. On he went, his horse starting and trembling, not having yet recovered from its fright. The rain was falling in torrents, and he was already wet through—no uncommon occurrence, however, for a squatter, who is in the saddle many hours every day of the year. Down it came, harder than ever. Another vivid flash, followed by a terrific clap of thunder, made his horse again start forward. He galloped on till an open space was reached; here, at all events, he might be secure from falling branches, though not from the lightning, which was darting in every direction.

He had almost lost hope of getting out of the wood that night. Wet as he was, he must camp out on the bare ground. He was searching for a spot where he might dismount and tether his horse, when again the animal started; this time, however, it was not at a flash of lightning. James looked round, when, about a dozen yards from him, he saw, as if endeavouring to conceal himself behind the gnarled stem of an aged gum tree of gigantic proportions, the very figure Johnstone had described to him the previous evening. At first he thought that his imagination must have deceived him; the light was uncertain, and his eyes had been dazzled by the lightning. Still, he could not be mistaken: there was the human face, the glaring eyeballs, the matted hair and beard, and the dress of skins and rags. The figure moved its arms and made threatening gestures at him. "I must know whether this is reality or imagination," he said to himself, again urging on his horse towards the tree under which the seeming figure stood. As he did so, the threatening gestures became more vehement, and, as he continued to advance, a loud, unearthly shriek rang through the forest, and the unhappy maniac, for such without doubt he was, fled away into its depths, his cries echoing amidst the trees till they grew faint in the distance. This incident did not contribute to make the prospect of camping out in that wild spot pleasant. Still, James Gilpin had no choice, and his mind was too well trained to allow him to be made anxious by unnecessary apprehensions. The only thing he dreaded was the possibility of the maniac returning, and, perhaps, should he drop asleep, committing some violence on him. Both rain and lightning had ceased, and having tethered his horse in a grassy spot, where the animal might find food, he bethought him of the possibility of lighting a fire. Under the trees there was no lack of fuel, and with the last remnant of daylight he collected enough to serve him till the morning. Under the lee side of the trees, also, he scraped together enough dry leaves and small twigs and bark to raise a blaze and dry the wet wood. He looked up very frequently, as was natural, to ascertain that the maniac was not near him. With flint, steel, and gunpowder he quickly raised a blaze; his kettle was boiling, his meat toasting, and his damper warming up, while his blanket and clothes were drying; and had it not been for the spectre he had seen, he would have been well content with his lot,—not that he much feared what the poor creature could do to him, but it was the feeling that at any moment he might rush out on him which was so painful. By the look of the sky he saw that the weather was still unsettled, and the state of the atmosphere, judging by his sensations, told him that there might still be more thunder and lightning. He consequently considered it imprudent to seek for greater shelter under the trees. His clothes and blankets were now tolerably dry, and having shifted the tether of his horse, that the animal might have fresh food, he wrapped himself up, with his feet to the fire and his head on his saddle-bags to seek that rest of which he stood so much in need.

W. H. G. Kingston

He, of course, intended to keep his eyes open, and turned in the direction where the poor maniac had disappeared. As might, however, have been expected, he closed them and fell fast asleep. Weariness made him sleep, but anxiety prevented him from sleeping soundly. He was dreaming, it seemed, all the time; and his dreams were painful and confused in the extreme. The strange figure of the maniac was constantly before him, while his unearthly cries resounded in his ears. His chief idea was that he was engaged in a desperate struggle to get out of some fearful difficulty—now swimming in a roaring torrent, now climbing a precipice with savage animals raging below, now flying for his life across a boundless plain; the maniac was mocking him on the banks of the stream, or present among the wild beasts, or following him with a troop of savages across the plain. A loud noise sounded in his ear. It was a peal of thunder. The storm was again raging with redoubled fury. He started up to secure his horse, lest the frightened animal should break loose and escape into the depths of the forest. He must have slept long, for a few glowing ashes only remained of his fire, which the rain would soon quench, unless a supply of fresh wood were added. He felt for some he had placed in readiness, and threw it on the ashes. As he did so, a vivid flash of lightning lit up the forest opening, and by its light he saw, with a gleaming axe uplifted in his hand, the wretched maniac stealthily approaching him. He sprang to his feet, seizing his rifle, when again all was darkness.

"Stand back, whoever you are, or I must fire!" he shouted, at the same time leaping on one side, away from the spot where he had been lying.

There was the sound of feet, as if a person was springing over the ground, a shriek, and the crash of a weapon descending. Yes, he was certain it had struck his saddle-bags. The next instant, the wood igniting on the fire, a flame burst forth, revealing the figure of the maniac retreating across the glade in the direction of the old tree, where he had at first appeared. He must have just reached it when another flash of lightning came down in a zigzag course from the very clouds overhead. It struck the huge tree, which was riven into several portions, and its knotted limbs scattered around. The thunder at the same moment crashed and rattled with almost terrific sound. He seized the tether rope of his horse, as the animal, having torn the pin from the ground, was about to dash off through the forest. The poor creature stood as his hand stroked its head, but trembled violently. He brought it up to the fire, looking round as he did so for his late assailant, but the maniac was nowhere to be seen. He had the greatest difficulty in keeping his horse quiet; for the storm continued raging as before, the rain came down in torrents, the wind howled and whistled, and the lightning flashed; the thunder roared and rattled, and the rending of boughs, and the crashing of falling trees was heard on every side, warning him of the danger of attempting to pass among them. As may be supposed, he did not again lie down: having saddled his horse and thrown his blanket over his shoulders, he employed the time in quieting the animal, throwing wood on his fire, and keeping a vigilant watch for the approach of the maniac. The most weary night must have an end. The storm ceased completely; the dawn came at last. He looked around. The sight which most attracted his attention was the blackened stump of that huge tree which had stood there the previous evening—the monarch of the forest glade. He approached it. Under one of the limbs lay a human form—it was the maniac's body; life was extinct. He examined the features. There could be no mistake; though haggard by starvation and exposure, and distorted by his violent death, he recognised them as those of the former overseer of Warragong, the outlaw Basham. A small black mark on one side of his head showed that he had been struck by the electric fluid, and that his death must have been instantaneous, and must have immediately followed the attempt on his life. To bury the body of the wretched man was impossible. All he could do was to drag the heavier boughs of the trees torn off by the storm over it and leave it thus entombed, and then to escape from the scene. The rising sun showed him the direction he should pursue, and in half an hour he was out of the wood, and had regained the track with which he was acquainted. He reached a station in time for breakfast, when he narrated to the occupant what had occurred, and learned from him that Basham had more than once been there asking for food.

A rest of a few hours restored James's strength; but instead of camping out as he had intended, he was glad to take shelter that night in another squatter's hut. It was thus that the traveller in those days was able to traverse the province from one end to the other, with the certainty of finding food and shelter, and a welcome at any hut where he might call. He was most cordially received at Prentiss Town, where he arrived late in the evening; but he went to a house of mourning. Old Mr Prentiss, under the belief that his losses were far greater than was the case, and that the whole country was about to be ruined, had sunk broken-hearted into the grave. He had trusted in riches, and they had failed him. An apathetic indifference to everything around him had seized his eldest son, who had the same belief in the ruin impending over the colony.

Notwithstanding this, there was sunlight in the dwelling: there could not fail to be so, James thought, where Fanny and Emily Prentiss were to be found. They received him as an old and valued friend, and expressed their sorrow that his brother could not have accompanied him. He naturally expected that they would complain of the dulness of the life they must now lead in the country, and regret all the gaieties and amusements they had left behind in Sydney; but, on the contrary, they seemed much pleased at having escaped from its unsatisfactory frivolities. Everything in the country delighted them, and they had no fear of no having ample occupation. They proposed to study the natural history of the district—the trees and flowers, the birds and insects, and the wild animals, of which there were not a few; then the farm would of itself afford ample occupation, along with the improvements in the house, into which they were about to move, on another part of the estate, where a garden was also to be formed. And there were also several settlers with wives and grown-up daughters, who lived somewhat far off, to be sure; but the young ladies were good horse-women, and thought little of a ride of thirty miles or so. There were likewise numerous families of the lower orders, who had no means of obtaining religious or secular instruction. Among these they circulated books and tracts, and would often stop and read the Word of God to those who were unable to read themselves. Thus every moment of each day was fully occupied. James Gilpin could not fail to admire the manner in which his young hostesses spent their time, or to discover how many objects of interest they had in common. Even under ordinary circumstances he would have been interested in them. As it was, the interest he felt increased the longer he remained in their society. He was of much use to Mr Henry Prentiss in arranging the affairs connected with the property; and at length, with new hopes and aspirations, he returned to Warragong. The arrangements for the purchase of the cattle and sheep were soon complete. The brothers did not even now lay out all their capital, but allowed a portion to remain in the bank to meet any unexpected demands. They had from the first been allowed a percentage on the increase of the stock under their charge; but this, owing to the mismanagement of the persons employed, and the depredations of Basham and his associates, had hitherto been small. The boiling-down process at length being no longer necessary, and the management in every department being greatly improved, the increase was so much more rapid than at first, that they found themselves, a few years after landing in Australia, the owners of very considerable flocks and herds, while no men in the district were more respected. Their visits to Prentiss Town became more and more frequent; sometimes one brother went, sometimes the other—as they were unwilling to leave the station together—and they both met with a reception which made them wish to return. The Prentiss Town property was now divided, and the house inhabited by Mr Henry Prentiss was considerably nearer to them than that of his elder brother. They also had secured some runs lower down the Warragong river; and having fixed on a site for a house in that direction, somewhat similar, but far more picturesque than the spot where the old hut stood, they built a hut which they could inhabit till their new residence could be erected, leaving Craven in charge of that up the stream. This change enabled them to leave their own abode early in the morning, and to reach that of Mr Prentiss before sunset. There was the house of a new settler about half-way, and several huts where refreshment could be obtained, so that their visits became still more frequent and expected. Even in the bush gossip is not impossible, and it became pretty generally reported that the two Mr Gilpins were about to marry the two daughters of Mr Henry Prentiss.

CHAPTER SIX

The Gilpins had not attained to the prosperous condition they enjoyed without persevering toil and constant exertion both of mind and body. Some stirring incidents had occurred; but, at the same time months passed by in a comparatively monotonous manner. Every day they were in the saddle, sometimes from morning till night; but however delightful that style of life may be—and that it has its attractions to most men there can be no doubt—men of educated minds must at times feel an almost insupportable weariness, and earnestly long for a change. There can be but little social intercourse; some suffer materially from the want of public worship and religious instruction, and all must feel its absence. Still, those who are fitted for a life in the bush, and have led it for any length of time, quit it generally with regret, and return to it with satisfaction.

Never had the Gilpins been more busy. Their house was nearly finished. It was rather large for two bachelors, to be sure; but their ideas must have expanded of late. They had much more assistance than formerly rendered by Craven, their most efficient and active overseer, and his assistant, Larry. No one would have recognised the dispirited, almost broken-hearted hut-keeper in the fine, active, intelligent man he had now become. Gentlemanly even in his poverty, he had always been. He now looked more fit to set a squadron in order, and lead them against the foe, than to keep sheep; yet to superintend the keeping of sheep he was well content. He had greatly enlarged and improved the old hut, having converted it indeed into a comfortable house, with a flower-garden in front and one for vegetables in the rear.

One of the greatest matters of interest to the bushman, who has loved relations in the old country, is the arrival of the post. Often with trembling, always with eager, hands the packets are opened; sometimes they give satisfaction, and afford subjects for pleasant conversation for many a day; but at others, and too often, they bring news to grieve the hearts of their readers. Such had been the case with the Gilpins, some time back, when a letter with a broad black border arrived, and told them of the death of a father they had so much reason to reverence and love. Several changes had taken place in their family circle. Their eldest brother had married; and their two sisters seemed doubtful, when they last heard from home, whether or not they should continue to reside with him.

The two brothers were sitting together in their nicely furni-shed dining-room. The dark wainscoting and the proportions of the apartment reminded them of the one they had loved so well in their far-off home in the old country. A dray had just arrived from the west, and Green made his appearance with the letter-bag in hand. Eagerly the contents were glanced over.

"Arthur, they are coming—both the dear girls, Jane and Susan—and Willie as an escort!" exclaimed James, in a tone of great satisfaction.

"Oh! it will be delightful. How pleased Fanny and Emily will be!" cried Arthur.

Indeed, no event could by possibility have caused the brothers more true pleasure; and, as may be supposed, it formed the subject for conversation for the remainder of the evening and for many evenings afterwards. Of course it was necessary for James to ride over to Prentiss Town to announce the event.

"As soon after they arrive as it can be arranged," was the reply made by Fanny to a question put to her during his visit. It seemed highly satisfactory, and was received with strong marks of gratitude.

When James returned home, Arthur was not happy till he could set off to Prentiss Town. He must have put a question to Emily, not unlike that which James put to Fanny.

"Perhaps the same day that my sister is," was her reply.

Not long after, James set off for Sydney. Arthur would gladly have gone also, but what with their own flocks and herds, and the numerous ones over which they had charge, it was, they thought, scarcely fair to Craven to leave him so long alone. Of late, too, there had been reports of wonderful discoveries of gold—nuggets to rival those of California; and some of the shepherds and stockmen had already gone off to the region where the gold was reported to have been found, and it was feared that others might follow. James had not been in Sydney since his first arrival in the country. The whole city was in a ferment. There was no doubt of the truth of the reports of the discovery of gold, not only in one, but in several directions. Nuggets of all sizes and heaps of gold-dust had already been brought in. The gold fever had commenced, and men of all ages, ranks, and professions were fitting themselves out with knapsacks, spades, washers, and other apparatus for the gold-fields. People were surprised that James took matters so calmly. "I prefer that others should dig for me—an occupation for which I never had a fancy, except for an hour or two in my garden in a morning," he answered. "If people rush out of the colony, as it is expected they will, the price of stock will rise very greatly, and I shall have ample fortune for all my wishes." It did rise, far higher than he expected, and he was not disappointed. His heart throbbed with anxiety as he went down to the harbour to visit the ship on board which his sisters had taken their passage. He singled them out among a large number of passengers, though they did not recognise the strongly built, bearded, and well-browned man as their brother, who had left them a fair, slight youth a few years before. News of the gold discoveries had reached England some time before the ship sailed, and a great number of her passengers were intended gold-diggers—a mixed and ill-matched assemblage, all inspired, however, with the one ruling passion, an eager to grow rich suddenly. There were young men—still mere lads—who had time before them to make themselves independent by steady industry; and old men who, it might be supposed, had little else to do than to prepare for another world. There were nominal representatives of all religious faiths, but drawn together to worship one god—Mammon, yet not as brethren, for each seemed eager to supplant the other. The Miss Gilpins told their brother that the universal subject of conversation during the voyage was gold, gold-digging, gold-washing, gold-scraping.

"Like the old man in the 'Pilgrim's Progress' with his muck-rake, always scraping with downcast looks, never gazing upwards," remarked James. "Ah! it is sad work; and yet, when a person gets down in the world, and feels the want of the wealth he once possessed, it must be a severe trial to him to prevent his mind from continually dwelling on the means by which he may regain it."

The greater number of the passengers were eager to set off

immediately for the diggings; and every vehicle to be found was secured at a high price, many giving promises of breaking down before half the journey was performed. Many talked of trudging it on foot; and of these, several of them never reached their destination, having either lost their way and died from fatigue and starvation in the bush, or being drowned when crossing some river, by being carried down by the current. The lions of Sydney were soon visited; and James, with his two sisters and young brother, set off in high spirits for Warragong. He had a lightly-built covered waggon, with strong springs—the best style of vehicle for travelling in the bush. The journey was performed, if not rapidly, yet with great ease and comfort; and there were so many objects of interest, all new to the strangers—the birds, beasts, reptiles, and scenery, the very look of the people, and the characters they met—that no one was weary. As may be supposed, they called at Prentiss Town on their way, and, of course, spent a few days there; and, naturally, Arthur arrived to escort them home. The daughters of the English farmer had been more practically brought up than the Australian young ladies, educated in a school in Sydney. They could teach them much connected with the dairy and numerous household duties, of which they had never heard. Not that the Miss Gilpins were, in the slightest degree, less refined or less educated than their new friends. Of course, the visit was to be returned; there was some joking, however, on that subject, which a stranger might not very clearly have understood. On the road, the party were met by Craven, well mounted, and dressed in the most approved fashion. He came, as in duty bound, to escort his friends' sisters to their new abode.

"And is this the hut you spoke of, dear brothers?" exclaimed the sisters, in the same voice. "What a delightful house! And this room, the very model of the dear old parlour. We are sure you intended it."

And Jane and Susan kissed their brothers, who were more than amply repaid by the happiness they felt for the years of toil they had endured, and all the exertions they had made to get the house ready. They had an idea that those sisters would not remain long under their roof, sorry though they would be to lose them; that is to say, not if their bachelor neighbours had a particle of good taste or judgment. Willie was delighted with everything. His great ambition was to become a first-rate stockman. He was rather young to begin active life; but he had made good use of his time at school, and he promised, when he left England, that he would not give up reading and study. The Gilpins had found the time pass quickly before the arrival of their sisters, they now found it pass still more quickly; and it was only by managing it with the greatest care that they could accomplish what they had to do. The Miss Gilpins entered warmly into all Fanny's and Emily's plans—which had, indeed, now become their brothers'—for giving religious instruction to the surrounding population, which had of late years considerably increased. Though many of the men went off to the diggings, the women remained, hoping to see them return, loaded with wealth. Not a hut nor a residence of any sort remained unvisited by these six active young missionaries, who left tracts or books wherever they went. They procured some Bibles from Sydney, and many a cottage, where the Word of God had never been heard, was supplied by them. They had great reason to believe that a blessing attended their efforts. They had often made application in Sydney for an appointed minister of the Gospel. One at length came, but he had a wide circuit, so that he could not come to any spot within the Sunday morning's journey more than six or eight times in the year. He went his rounds, preaching on weekdays, from station to station, and holding a service every evening where he rested. Such is the only human agency by which spiritual life can be maintained in the wide-scattered sheep and stock stations in Australia, and it behoves all those connected with that magnificent land, who love the Lord Jesus Christ, to aid in sending missionaries of the Gospel through its length and breadth. There are many who have scarcely ever heard the glad tidings of salvation; many have passed away, sunk almost in heathen darkness. At length, a regular place of worship was built, to the satisfaction of many, which satisfaction was by no means decreased by an interesting event which took place there shortly afterwards, namely, the marriages of Jane and Arthur Gilpin. It would be difficult to find a more united, contented, and happy family than that now dwelling at Warragong, and certainly, if steady, persevering, industry and uprightness of conduct should be rewarded, the Gilpins richly deserved their success. Sam Green, too, had followed his young master's example, and had taken to himself as a wife the eldest daughter of his old acquaintance, Sykes, the former coachman of Mr Henry Prentiss, who had followed his master into the country, and settled near him. Larry Killock won the heart of another daughter; but, although Mr Sykes had himself come out at the Government expense, he objected to the alliance, because Larry was not yet entirely a free man. Larry was, however, able to prove that his crime was having joined some popular outbreak; and being at length freed completely from bondage, his wishes were no longer opposed, and he settled down near the friends to whom he had, with good reason, become so warmly attached.

CHAPTER SEVEN

Some time had passed since the events just mentioned. It was winter, not Christmas, however, but the period which in England is considered the warmest and sunniest in the year. Frost and snow are not looked for, but the wind blows from the cold south, and rain comes down in plentiful showers, filling the water-holes, and turning the sluggish streams into roaring torrents.

One evening, as Arthur and Willie were riding homewards from a distant station, their course not far from the Warragong river, a cry reached their ears.

"It is some one shouting for help!" exclaimed Arthur. "From what direction does it come? Listen!"

"From up the stream!" cried Willie, spurring on his horse.

"Stay! there's a man in the river," said Arthur; "he is floating down. We may pass him if we don't take care."

They rode directly down to the bank of the now rapid river. Every stockman rides with a rope attached to his saddle. They looked out anxiously as they now rode up the stream. Again the cry was heard, but fainter though near; and through the thickening gloom of evening a man was seen clinging to a log, which was borne swiftly down the current. He had lost all power of guiding it, and from the way his head hung down, it was evident that his strength was exhausted, and that he must soon drop off and sink. To leap from their horses and to secure them to a tree was the work of a moment.

"Here, hold one end, Willie! I think I can reach him!" cried Arthur, binding the two ropes together, and fastening one end round his own waist.

Throwing off his coat, and without waiting for any expostulation from Willie, he plunged into the stream, and swam boldly out towards the drowning man. The whirling eddies of the torrent bore the log along, now carrying it towards one side of the river, now towards the other. This much increased the difficulty of reaching it. The man clinging to it had still sufficient consciousness to be aware of the effort made to save him, but had no strength to help himself. Arthur had swum out very nearly to the extent of which the rope would allow, and yet he feared that he should not reach the man. He doubted whether he should be strong enough to return to the shore without the aid of the rope.

"Stretch out your arms, Willie; give me all the rope you can, but don't fall in. In mercy take care!" he shouted.

Willie stood on the very edge of the bank uncoiling the whole of the rope, and keeping only the end in his hands. He dreaded lest, his feet slipping, he should be dragged in himself; and though he did not fear for himself, he knew that, if he was dragged in, Arthur would in all probability be lost. He found that he could not stand still either, but had to move down the stream, as his brother was swept on by the current. "If it is difficult to hold him now, what will it be when he grasps the drowning man?" he thought. He would have

W. H. G. Kingston

shouted for help had he believed that any one was near to afford it. Arthur, meantime, saw the drowning man approaching. An eddy seemed to be carrying him off towards the opposite bank. Should he venture to swim across without the rope? Had he a right to run so great a risk of losing his life, and bring grief and sorrow to the heart of his young wife? He prayed for strength and aid. He was about to loose himself from the rope, when again the log was whirled near him. The moment for the greatest exertion had arrived. He sprang forward. His right hand grasped the drowning man, but the log on which he floated escaped from his hold, and was borne onwards by the current. As he caught the man, the spring he made and the additional weight almost over-balanced Willie, who was on the point of falling into the water, when he found himself close to a young tree, of the willow tribe, bending over the stream. He grasped it with his left hand, hauling with all his might till he drew in a sufficient length of the rope to pass it round the stem. His dread was lest his brother should sink before he could reach the shore. He then feared that the man for whom Arthur had risked so much might be torn from his grasp before he could get him in. The fact of the willow growing there showed that there was a permanent water-hole at the spot, and that, therefore, the depth must be considerable. He dragged in the rope slowly, for Arthur seemed scarcely able to support his burden. "Keep— keep up, brother!" he cried out, considering whether he should not make the rope fast and jump in to help him. Just then he discovered that the current itself was doing what he wished; scarcely had he secured the rope than Arthur was swept close up to the bank. He sprang on to help him. The bank, happily, shelved, and together they dragged the nearly drowned man to the shore. He was dressed as a labourer, and his rough hands showed that he was accustomed to hard work. It was too dark to distinguish his features. After they had rubbed him for some time, he gave signs of life; and on his further recovering they placed him on Willie's horse, and, supporting him on either side, led him up to the house, which was about half a mile distant. The stranger scarcely spoke all the way; indeed, he was but partially recovered from the effects of his immersion. The ladies of the family, who had been expecting them at an earlier hour, ran out as they reached the house. Emily hurried off her husband to change his wet clothes; while Willie, briefly describing how bravely his brother had behaved, conducted the stranger to his room, that he might go to bed, while dry garments were got for him and some hot potation was prepared. Had he been of the highest instead, apparently, of the lowest rank, he could not have been more kindly treated. Willie was delighted to be of use, and having collected some clothes from his brother's wardrobe, brought them to the stranger, who, having taken the remedies prescribed for him, insisted on getting up.

"Why, whose house am I in?" exclaimed the stranger, his eye falling on the mark of some of the linen brought for him.

His young attendant told him.

"Then you surely must be little Willie Gilpin!" cried the stranger; "and that fine fellow who jumped into the river and pulled me out is Arthur, and those are your sisters. I thought I knew their faces."

"And who are you?" asked Willie.

"An old friend, though I think it likely a forgotten one," answered the stranger. "Do not say that I know your people. If they recollect me, well and good; if not, it matters little: I am not worth recollecting."

It was evident that the stranger did not belong to the rank of life his appearance had at first betokened. James, who had been at a distance, now arriving, came to the door, and invited him in to supper. The stranger followed him, and with a bow to the ladies, which was certainly not like that of a mere countryman, was about to take a seat at table, when Arthur entered. The stranger's colour mounted to his cheeks as he said—

"I am indebted to you, sir, for my life, and I am most thankful, as it enables me to enjoy the present society, though I fear my life is not worth the risk you ran to save it."

Arthur had been earnestly examining the countenance of the stranger while he was speaking. "I thought so," he exclaimed, coming round to him and taking his hand; "Mark Withers, of Wallington?"

"The same, though somewhat wiser; rather further down the hill than when we parted," returned the stranger. "But I'll own it does my heart good to meet so many old friends together."

Kind and warm greetings saluted the wanderer; his heart softened, and for a time he laid aside his cynical, discontented manner. The well-furnished rooms, the handsome arrangements of the supper-table, and the servants in attendance, all spoke of ample means. A feeling of jealousy might possibly have passed through his heart as he made these observations. He remarked, however, when left alone with the brothers, "Well, you fellows seem to have fallen on your feet; and I'm heartily glad of it, indeed I am."

"We have been working pretty hard, though," said James; and, after giving a brief sketch of their career in the colony, he asked, "And you, Withers, I hope that you have got a comfortable home in Australia somewhere."

"Home!" exclaimed Withers; "I haven't a wigwam I can call my own, and my whole property consists in the damp duds I had on my back when I pulled them off in Willie's room."

"Where have you been, then, Mark, all this time?" asked Arthur.

"Been! why, my dear fellow, all round the world, exemplifying the truth of the saying, that 'a rolling stone gathers no moss.' My father did not much fancy my giving up his business; and indeed I had to take French leave at last, and then write and ask his forgiveness. He told me, in reply, that I was a graceless vagabond; but that I might follow my own devices, if I was so minded, without opposition, though without help from him. I fancied that my own devices were full of wisdom, so resolved to follow them. I had fallen in with a man bound for the Cape of Good Hope Colony, and, listening to his representations, agreed to accompany him. Out to the Cape I went, but soon discovered that a farm-life was not to my taste; and so, meeting with some sporting companions, I spent my time in shooting elephants and lions, and other beasts of the forests and mountains of that wonderful land. As my expenses at this sort of work were far greater than my profits, I spent, in time, all the money I possessed, and had at length to engage as a labourer on a property of which, on first landing, I might have become the owner. This was not what I had bargained for; and hearing that fortunes were to be made rapidly in South Australia, I saved enough money to carry me to Cape Town, where I found a ship calling in on her way to that colony. I shipped on board her to work my passage; but finding the work I had to do and the treatment I had received very far from my taste, I resolved never again, if I could help it, to place myself in the same position. I found, on reaching Adelaide, that if fortunes were to be made in a hurry, they were to be lost still more rapidly—not that I had myself any opportunity of making the experiment I tried all sorts of plans which I thought would prove short roads to what I so much desired—to become rich; but, somehow or other, none of them proved satisfactory. At length I had struck out something new which would, I really believe, have been a great success, when the news of the wonderful discoveries of gold in California reached the colony. Wonderful to relate, I had made enough money to pay my passage, which I took on board one of the first vessels sailing for those regions I considered myself wonderfully fortunate to get there, for I had now no longer the slightest doubt of success. San Francisco was already a wonderful place. Everybody on board hastened to the shore as soon as we entered the harbour, and in the course of two or three days the whole of the crew, except the captain and first mate, had deserted the ship. The central part of the city consisted at that time chiefly of lodging-houses, gambling-houses, and houses of entertainment. The lodging-houses, fast as they could be put up, were crowded, and were of the most wretched description. The best to which I could gain admission was a long barn-like edifice, with bunks or berths like those on board a ship, arranged along on either side with straw, hay, or leaves as a mattress, and a horsecloth as a coverlet. The gambling-houses were the most attractive. There was music gratis, and spirits without limitation for all who chose to play. I felt sure that I should make my fortune in that way. How was I to get enough to stake? I must work. I found no difficulty in obtaining employment as a labourer at high wages. In a short time I had saved about twenty dollars. I walked into the largest gambling-house, with my few dollars jingling in my pockets. The hall was brilliantly lighted. It was hung with coloured silk or calico, and adorned with mirrors and pictures. There was a gallery with a band of music, and a bar where all sorts of viands could be obtained. There were small tables for cards on either side, and several larger tables in the centre, at which sat the bankers, the professional gamblers, the owners or renters of the saloon. I walked up to one of these tables and staked five of my hardly gained dollars against a thousand or so, and won. I won again and again, until I found myself the owner of twenty thousand dollars. I had never been so rich in my life, but yet it was not a sum which would allow me to leave off. I played on all night, losing and regaining; and at length, when the saloon was closed, I had but a quarter of my first winning remaining. This would never do. I determined to go the next day, and I persuaded myself that if I could win as much as I had done the first night, I would never bet on a card again. I returned to that hall of horrors—for so it was, in spite of its gilding and mirrors and music. The haggard, pallid countenances of the professional players, almost Satanic in their calmness; the excited, eager looks of those who had come in the hopes, by staking their all, of clearing themselves from difficulties, or, by rapidly acquiring wealth; of being able to return to their far-distant homes! To a considerable number, I believe, the scene was thoroughly distasteful; and yet, infatuated folly led them, as it did me, there. I won at first; but fortune turned against me, and I went on losing rapidly. If I staked high, I lost; if low, it was the same. Every instant I expected to have my first good luck come back, till I discovered that, to the very last dollar, my pocket was cleared out. But I saw a terrible sight that evening—I spare you the particulars—the suicide of a poor young Englishman, who, like me, had lost every shilling he had. I trembled lest I should be tempted to commit a like act; for I found that hardly a week passed by but some wretched victim of gaming thus plunged into a fearful eternity, while numbers took to drinking hard, and brought themselves speedily to the grave. Sickened for the time of gambling, I worked hard again, till I had saved enough to take me up to the diggings. I found one of my shipmates about to start. We agreed to go together. We were bound to each other, not by mutual regard, but that we required companionship, and believed we could trust each other. I do not much like to think of all the hardships we underwent. We had some distance to go up the river, on the crowded deck of a vessel; then, with our packs on our backs, we commenced the toilsome part of our journey, over mountain and valley, across rivers and plains, on the highlands, exposed to sharp winds, which pierced bitterly through our light clothes, while on the plains we were scorched with the fierce rays of the unclouded sun. A large party had collected at the foot of a rugged mountain. Before us lay a plain of vast extent, which must be crossed. We had heard that there was a scarcity of water. Some had filled their water-skins and jars and kegs; others laughed at the notion of not being able to go a few hours without water, even should we not find any; and some carried flasks filled with rum or brandy, boasting that that was the best stuff for quenching thirst I never felt greater heat in the tropics; the air was filled with the finest dust, which got down our throats, stopped our nostrils, and filled up the pores of our already parched skins. The first night we stopped for very weariness—no water was to be found. Those who had some would not part with a drop to their comrades: they might want it themselves. All night the wolves howled round us, as if scenting their prey. There were reports, too, that hostile Indians had been seen; and several times the camp was aroused by an alarm that the redskins were on us. The next day, when the sun rose, the sky was cloudless, and there was not a breath of wind. Greater than ever was the heat, and more intense the thirst of those who had brought no water. I had a small flask full; but though I kept wetting my lips occasionally, I suffered dreadfully. Almost certain destruction would be the lot of those who dropped behind; yet, one by one, several poor wretches sunk down exhausted, in vain imploring the rest to carry them on. Sad were their cries; but our breasts were steeled against their appeals. We had our own safety to consult, and the gold mines were before us. Among those who sunk down were several who carried flasks of spirits. Our guides declared that we should reach water before sunset. This kept up the spirits of the stronger men. They were mistaken, or had purposely deceived us to encourage us to proceed. Again we slept on the burning sand, with our pistols in our hands, and our water-bottles under our heads, ready at a moment's notice to defend ourselves against either Indians, wolves, or our own companions, who, tempted by thirst, might endeavour to steal the water we found so precious. The howling of the wolves in the distance, and the groans, and often the imprecations of those suffering from thirst, drove away sleep; and I, with others, started up to reach the river, which we were assured was not more than fifteen miles off. In four or five hours it might be reached. We pushed on at a rapid rate, our mules following willingly, instinct telling them that relief was at hand. The green trees appeared in sight, and the water, bright and limpid, was seen between them. We hurried on—men and animals together rushing into the stream, the men lapping the water up like dogs, and dipping their whole bodies in without even stopping to pull off any of their clothes. It is a wonder the sudden change from heat to cold did not kill some of us; but the fact is, that our pores were so completely closed up with dust that the bath, by removing the dirt, allowed the perspiration to escape and saved us from fever. A few turns in the sun soon dried our garments, and then delightful indeed was it to throw ourselves on the grass, in the shade of the tall trees, and to rest after our fatigue. One man proposed that we should load our mules with water and go back for our poor comrades who had dropped in the desert, if the caravan would camp for a couple of days; but the proposal was instantly negatived with derision.

"What! did he forget that we were bound for the diggings? Lose two whole days which might be employed in collecting the gold of which we were so eagerly in search! Scarcely had our companions came up than on we pushed. The diggings were at hand; the nearer we got to them, the more eager we

W. H. G. Kingston

became to commence work. We reached at last the principal diggings. It was a fearfully wild spot—mountains on all sides, almost destitute of trees, with the river running between them; the ground in every direction was full of burrows, as if the habitation of rabbits; but the chief work was going forward by the banks of the river, where hundreds of men were labouring away from morn till night with very varied success. My partner and I set up a hut; it was a wretched affair, but not worse than many others; then we turned to with eager, beating hearts. We dug and washed hour after hour, but, toil as we might, we had not, at the end of the day, obtained more than would pay our expenses; sometimes not so much. We toiled on. We had no choice; we must find gold or starve. With the cold wind descending from the mountains at night, and the chill fogs; the hot sun by day striking down on our heads while we stood up to our knees in water—no wonder that all suffered more or less from ague and fever. Many died from disease, some went mad, some committed suicide. There was no one to care for them, no one to mourn them; bowie-knives were in constant requisition, murders frequent. One day I heard shots fired, and ran to see what was occurring. Some strangers, that is, natives of various countries, had trespassed on the ground claimed by a company of Americans. Without giving any warning, the latter assembled and fired on the new-comers, killing several; then rushing on them with bowie-knives, axes, and revolvers, they desperately wounded or killed several more, putting the rest to flight. 'There, I guess they'll not try it on again,' I heard one of the victors say, as he kicked the dead body of one of the conquered party. I could describe many other similar scenes. At night we always slept with our pistols under our pillows, and our knives at our sides, ready to start up at a moment's notice. Several successful diggers were murdered for the sake of their wealth, and others were cut off by Indians, while prospecting beyond the chief diggings. Altogether, I don't think that any place on earth could have been more like Pandemonium than were those Californian diggings at the time I was there, for I have not mentioned half of its horrors and abominations. I resolved to get out of them. An unexpected run of success gave me the means; the news of the discovery of gold in Australia expedited my movements. My partner agreed to share my fortunes. We got back to San Francisco, though not without great hazard of losing our gold and our lives, and got on board a ship bound across the Pacific to this country. The ship, however, being caught in a gale off this coast, drove on shore, when half the crew and passengers lost their lives—my partner among them—while I only saved my life and the clothes on my back. I had learned by this time not to be surprised at any misfortune which might overtake me. I was far better off than in California, for I was among country-men, I begged my way up to the diggings, or rather I had not to beg it, for I was passed along from station to station. I was much better off, too, at the diggings than I had been in California, for I was now one of the ruling faction; and, though things were bad enough in some respects, people were generally civilised and humane, compared to gold-diggers I had met on the other side of the globe. My luck, however, was much the same. All I could do was to keep body and soul together, till at last I had to come to the conclusion that I was not cut out for a gold-digger. On my way up to the diggings, I had rested at a station owned by an old gentleman, who seemed to take an interest in me. At all events, as I was going away, he promised to receive me when I got tired of gold-digging, if I would come back to him, and to put me in the way of making my fortune. Utterly disgusted with my ill-success as gold-digger, I bethought myself of him, and was on my way to his abode, when, on attempting to cross your river, I was carried off my feet, and should have become food for fish or water-rats had it not been for your courage, Arthur and Willie; and I can say, with sincerity, that you deserve great credit for it. As to thanking

W. H. G. Kingston

you, I do not fancy that thanks from such a wretched vagabond as I am are worth anything, and so I'll say nothing about that."

"We are too glad that we have succeeded in saving your life, old friend, to care about thanks," said Arthur. "And now you are here, we hope that you will stay and try if you cannot follow our occupation. It is the one that succeeds best in Australia in the long run, depend upon it."

Mark Withers said that he would think about the matter; but the next morning he declared his intention of proceeding to the farm of the old gentleman, a Mr Elton, who had invited him to his house before he went up to the diggings. "The fact is," observed Mark, "I have an idea that he intended to leave me his property, and that would not be an unpleasant way of making a fortune, you'll allow."

"It would be a way of getting one, certainly," observed James; "though I doubt if your expectations will be realised; and I think that you would enjoy it far more if you make it yourself by honest industry."

"Every man to his taste," said Mark, with a careless laugh; "if I fail in my expectations, I can but try on plodding industry at last, you know, and little harm will be done."

"It is difficult to stop a rolling stone when it has gained an impetus downhill," said James; "remember that, Mark. However, I can only say that my brothers and I shall be glad to welcome you back, should you find yourself mistaken in your hopes, and to find some employment for you which will put you in the way of becoming independent in the end."

In so great a hurry was Mark to assure himself that he should obtain the expected fortune from Mr Elton, that he insisted on setting forth on his journey the next day. He did not object, however, to borrow a horse and a few pounds from his old friends. This he did with the air of a man conferring rather than receiving a favour. When Craven, who arrived soon afterwards, heard of this latter circumstance, he predicted that the face of Mr Mark Withers would not be again seen at Warragong, unless he might have the assurance to return and borrow more.

Charles Craven had become a very constant visitor of late at Warragong. By his intelligence, activity, and knowledge of mankind, he had contributed greatly to the prosperity of the Gilpins own property, as well as to that committed to their charge. They had obtained permission to make over a considerable portion of the latter to his management, so that he had now a comfortable, if not a handsome, income. There seemed to be no doubt that he admired Miss Gilpin, though he had not proposed to her. Perhaps he considered that she was indifferent to him, or regarded him merely as a valued friend of her brothers.

Nothing had been heard of Mark Withers since his departure. One evening a horseman was seen approaching the house, dressed in rough bush fashion; and soon afterwards, into the room where the ladies were seated, walked Mark himself. He had assumed a careless independent swagger, peculiarly distasteful to those into whose society he had introduced himself.

"Your brothers were right!" he exclaimed, throwing himself into a chair. "Old Elton was a humbug. He has cheated me abominably. Got me to labour for him, and then laughed in my face when I told him why I had done so; telling me that, as I worked for love, I required no wages; and that, as I was not worth my salt, he should give me none. However, here I am, not much the worse for the adventure, with a few months experience of bush life, and ready to become your brothers' chief stockman, or overseer, or anything they like to put me to, not derogatory to the character of a gentleman."

The Miss Gilpins and their sisters-in-law would have been inclined to laugh at this speech, had it not been for the impudence of Mark's looks and tone. On the arrival of the gentlemen he softened his manner; and James and Arthur, ever kind and thoughtful, began at once to consider how they could employ their old companion, so that he might not feel the weight of his obligation to them. He decided that he would be employed as a stockman, without considering his fitness for the occupation, but preferring to ride about on a good horse to walking on foot or sitting in the house with account-books before him. He acquitted himself, however, more to his employers' satisfaction than they had expected. He learned to ride and manage his horse well; and by the time he had gained a knowledge of the country, he had attained many of the requisites of a good stockman. He showed no inclination, however, to consider himself of the rank of one, but, assuming on his early friendship with the Gilpins, was constantly appearing at the house, and at length it became tolerably evident that he proposed to better his fortunes by marrying one of the Miss Gilpins. Jane had reason to believe that she was honoured by his preference. Suddenly, after this discovery, Craven ceased to pay his visits at the house as usual, or, if he came, went only to the business room, and declined stopping to luncheon or dinner. Whether or not Jane was in any way concerned at this, she let no one discover. Mark came oftener than ever, boasting that he should soon become a stockholder on a large scale, and that he intended to introduce great improvements in the management of cattle in Australia.

Where cattle are so apt to stray, as in the Australian bush, herds of different proprietors may occasionally get mingled, and therefore it is necessary to brand them carefully. When this operation is to be performed, the animals are driven into a pound. Ropes are then cast over the horns and legs of the bullock to be first marked, he is thrown to the ground, and the hot iron is applied. This is often a work of no little danger; for when a young bull, who has been roaming at liberty since his calfhood, finds himself thus treated, he is apt to turn on his tormentors, and to attempt to retaliate. A considerable mob of cattle had to be branded at Warragong, and all the hands who could be collected were employed in driving them into the pound. To get them there was difficult; to hold them quiet while being marked was still more so. One young and very powerful bull had resisted all the attempts made to catch him, when Mark Withers—who at that instant caught sight of the Miss Gilpins riding by— declared that he could manage the animal; and, leaping over the paling, lasso in hand, approached it with unexpected hardihood. The animal's rage appeared excited to an ungovernable pitch at seeing him, and, lowering his head with a loud roar, he dashed towards him. While attempting to spring on one side, the unfortunate man's foot slipped, and before he could recover himself, he was transfixed by the animal's horns. The bull then, lifting up his head, bore his victim as if in triumph round and round the pound. In vain Withers struggled to release himself, and shrieked for help. James and Arthur and Willie, followed by several men, leaped into the pound, regardless of the risk they ran of being set on by other animals.

"Oh! horrible! Save him! save him!" simultaneously cried the Miss Gilpins, who had ridden up.

At that moment Craven, who heard their cry, rode up, and, seeing the state of affairs, ordered the gate to be opened, and dashed in. The next instant he had thrown the lasso over the bull's head, clearing the man, and while he drew it tight round the creature's neck, the rest of the party came up and were able to get theirs round his legs and to bring him to the ground. Mark breathed, but had received some severe injuries. Whether they might prove fatal it was difficult to say.

"Oh! Mr Craven, we are indeed grateful for the way in which you released that poor man from his horrible position," said Jane, in a sweet, yet unfaltering voice, as, on riding out of the pound, Craven bowed stiffly to the sisters.

He looked at Jane's countenance earnestly, and then rode up alongside her horse.

"I have some slight surgical skill, perhaps I may be of service," he said quietly.

Withers was being carried at this time towards the house.

"Oh! try what you can do. My brothers will be most thankful. It would be dreadful were he to die in his present, as I fear, unprepared state," she replied.

Craven drew a deep breath. Susan echoed her sister's words. They were approaching the house.

Craven's skill was not very great, but he was gentle and patient, and contributed to relieve the sufferings of the injured man. Many hours passed before the surgeon, who had been sent for, arrived. In the mean time, Craven was as assiduous in his attention as he could have been had Mark been his dearest friend. The surgeon would not pronounce a decided opinion as to the case. Though the injuries were severe, if the man's constitution was good he might recover, but if not, they would probably prove fatal. James, as a true friend, felt that it was his duty to tell Mark the truth.

The injured man groaned and muttered, "Yes, it was good; but I have done my best to destroy it."

James spoke to him earnestly, and urged him, without delay, to make his peace with God, through the only means open to sinful man—the blood of His dear Son.

Mark listened, but a veil seemed on his understanding. "The fact is, old fellow, I haven't thought about the matter, and I would rather not now," he replied. "I don't intend to die just yet, if I can help it; and who knows but what I may take up your notions of things, and become as good as you are? You mean me well, I know you do; but just let me alone."

But a faithful man is faithful in all things. Arthur persevered, and at length a perceptible change took place in Mark's manner when he spoke of sacred matters. The fear of death in him became great. More than once Arthur heard him muttering to himself those awful words: HEREAFTER! ETERNITY! At length the surgeon began to speak more favourably of Mark's condition. He thought he would recover, he said, but would be a cripple to the end of his life. It was a heavy blow to Mark, and caused him many bitter tears, although it was evident that it was a wonderful relief to his mind to be told that God had given him time for repentance, and not cut him off in the midst of his sins. Arthur was by his bedside continually, and it filled him with deep joy to be able to believe that Mark was a changed man. He spoke penitently, sorrowfully, of the past, but cheerfully and hopefully of the future. One day, as he was lying on a sofa, to which he had been lifted from his bed, he said to Arthur, "I remember long ago, in the old country, Arthur, when you and I were discussing what was the object in life most worthy of our aim, I thought wealth, for the sake of spending it on pleasure—on myself. I could not make out exactly what your aim was; but you and your brothers seem to me to have got all you can desire to make life pleasant, while I have lost all I had, and gained nothing."

"I held, I believe, that all we should aim at is to do our duty, and that openings for the employment of our energies will always be found for us," answered Arthur. "We certainly have found this to be true in our own case."

"Yes, that you have," said Mark, without, however, any bitterness in his tone. "I should have called it luck once, but I won't now. I will try, by God's mercy, poor helpless creature that I am, to find some means of usefulness, that so I may not be a mere cumberer of the earth, but may repay in any way that may offer itself some little portion of the kindness of my benefactors."

The Gilpins had truly been fruitful fig trees. All they undertook prospered.

Far and wide they were a blessing to their neighbours, for as such they looked upon all those—rich or poor—whom they could reach.

Through their efforts and instrumentality the glad tidings of great joy were carried to all around them, many of whom would never otherwise have heard the Gospel sound.

The contrast between the career of the brothers and their quondam friend was great, but not greater than will usually be found between those who set the Lord always before their eyes, and seek him early while yet He may be found, and those who turn aside from His ways and refuse to follow them.

Craven declared that it was impossible any one could reap more benefit from his friends than he had. It seemed probable, indeed, that, but for them, he would have remained a hut-keeper to the end of his days. As it was, he became not merely an upright man in the eye of his fellow-men, but also a sincere Christian. He married Jane Gilpin, and with this event we close our narrative.

THE END

W. H. G. Kingston

ABOUT THE AUTHOR

William Henry Giles Kingston (1814 - 1880), writer of tales for boys, born in London, but spent much of his youth in Oporto, where his father was a merchant.

His first book, The Circassian Chief, appeared in 1844. His first book for boys, Peter the Whaler, was published in 1851, and had such success that he retired from business and devoted himself entirely to the production of this kind of literature, in which his popularity was deservedly great; and during 30 years he wrote upwards of 130 tales, including The Three Midshipmen (1862), The Three Lieutenants (1874), The Three Commanders (1875), The Three Admirals (1877), Digby Heathcote, etc.

He also conducted various papers, including The Colonist, and Colonial Magazine and East India Review. He was also interested in emigration, volunteering, and various philanthropic schemes. For services in negotiating a commercial treaty with Portugal he received a Portuguese knighthood, and for his literary labours a Government pension.

Choose from Thousands of 1stWorldLibrary Classics By

A. M. Barnard
Ada Leverson
Adolphus William Ward
Aesop
Agatha Christie
Alexander Aaronsohn
Alexander Kielland
Alexandre Dumas
Alfred Gatty
Alfred Ollivant
Alice Duer Miller
Alice Turner Curtis
Alice Dunbar
Allen Chapman
Alleyne Ireland
Ambrose Bierce
Amelia E. Barr
Amory H. Bradford
Andrew Lang
Andrew McFarland Davis
Andy Adams
Angela Brazil
Anna Alice Chapin
Anna Sewell
Annie Besant
Annie Hamilton Donnell
Annie Payson Call
Annie Roe Carr
Annonaymous
Anton Chekhov
Archibald Lee Fletcher
Arnold Bennett
Arthur C. Benson
Arthur Conan Doyle
Arthur M. Winfield
Arthur Ransome
Arthur Schnitzler
Arthur Train
Atticus
B.H. Baden-Powell
B. M. Bower
B. C. Chatterjee
Baroness Emmuska Orczy
Baroness Orczy
Basil King
Bayard Taylor
Ben Macomber
Bertha Muzzy Bower
Bjornstjerne Bjornson

Booth Tarkington
Boyd Cable
Bram Stoker
C. Collodi
C. E. Orr
C. M. Ingleby
Carolyn Wells
Catherine Parr Traill
Charles A. Eastman
Charles Amory Beach
Charles Dickens
Charles Dudley Warner
Charles Farrar Browne
Charles Ives
Charles Kingsley
Charles Klein
Charles Hanson Towne
Charles Lathrop Pack
Charles Romyn Dake
Charles Whibley
Charles Willing Beale
Charlotte M. Braeme
Charlotte M. Yonge
Charlotte Perkins Stetson
Clair W. Hayes
Clarence Day Jr.
Clarence E. Mulford
Clemence Housman
Confucius
Coningsby Dawson
Cornelis DeWitt Wilcox
Cyril Burleigh
D. H. Lawrence
Daniel Defoe
David Garnett
Dinah Craik
Don Carlos Janes
Donald Keyhoe
Dorothy Kilner
Dougan Clark
Douglas Fairbanks
E. Nesbit
E. P. Roe
E. Phillips Oppenheim
E. S. Brooks
Earl Barnes
Edgar Rice Burroughs
Edith Van Dyne
Edith Wharton

Edward Everett Hale
Edward J. O'Biren
Edward S. Ellis
Edwin L. Arnold
Eleanor Atkins
Eleanor Hallowell Abbott
Eliot Gregory
Elizabeth Gaskell
Elizabeth McCracken
Elizabeth Von Arnim
Ellem Key
Emerson Hough
Emilie F. Carlen
Emily Bronte
Emily Dickinson
Enid Bagnold
Enilor Macartney Lane
Erasmus W. Jones
Ernie Howard Pie
Ethel May Dell
Ethel Turner
Ethel Watts Mumford
Eugene Sue
Eugenie Foa
Eugene Wood
Eustace Hale Ball
Evelyn Everett-green
Everard Cotes
F. H. Cheley
F. J. Cross
F. Marion Crawford
Fannie E. Newberry
Federick Austin Ogg
Ferdinand Ossendowski
Fergus Hume
Florence A. Kilpatrick
Fremont B. Deering
Francis Bacon
Francis Darwin
Frances Hodgson Burnett
Frances Parkinson Keyes
Frank Gee Patchin
Frank Harris
Frank Jewett Mather
Frank L. Packard
Frank V. Webster
Frederic Stewart Isham
Frederick Trevor Hill
Frederick Winslow Taylor

Friedrich Kerst
Friedrich Nietzsche
Fyodor Dostoyevsky
G.A. Henty
G.K. Chesterton
Gabrielle E. Jackson
Garrett P. Serviss
Gaston Leroux
George A. Warren
George Ade
Geroge Bernard Shaw
George Cary Eggleston
George Durston
George Ebers
George Eliot
George Gissing
George MacDonald
George Meredith
George Orwell
George Sylvester Viereck
George Tucker
George W. Cable
George Wharton James
Gertrude Atherton
Gordon Casserly
Grace E. King
Grace Gallatin
Grace Greenwood
Grant Allen
Guillermo A. Sherwell
Gulielma Zollinger
Gustav Flaubert
H. A. Cody
H. B. Irving
H.C. Bailey
H. G. Wells
H. H. Munro
H. Irving Hancock
H. R. Naylor
H. Rider Haggard
H. W. C. Davis
Haldeman Julius
Hall Caine
Hamilton Wright Mabie
Hans Christian Andersen
Harold Avery
Harold McGrath
Harriet Beecher Stowe
Harry Castlemon
Harry Coghill
Harry Houidini

Hayden Carruth
Helent Hunt Jackson
Helen Nicolay
Hendrik Conscience
Hendy David Thoreau
Henri Barbusse
Henrik Ibsen
Henry Adams
Henry Ford
Henry Frost
Henry James
Henry Jones Ford
Henry Seton Merriman
Henry W Longfellow
Herbert A. Giles
Herbert Carter
Herbert N. Casson
Herman Hesse
Hildegard G. Frey
Homer
Honore De Balzac
Horace B. Day
Horace Walpole
Horatio Alger Jr.
Howard Pyle
Howard R. Garis
Hugh Lofting
Hugh Walpole
Humphry Ward
Ian Maclaren
Inez Haynes Gillmore
Irving Bacheller
Isabel Cecilia Williams
Isabel Hornibrook
Israel Abrahams
Ivan Turgenev
J.G.Austin
J. Henri Fabre
J. M. Barrie
J. M. Walsh
J. Macdonald Oxley
J. R. Miller
J. S. Fletcher
J. S. Knowles
J. Storer Clouston
J. W. Duffield
Jack London
Jacob Abbott
James Allen
James Andrews
James Baldwin

James Branch Cabell
James DeMille
James Joyce
James Lane Allen
James Lane Allen
James Oliver Curwood
James Oppenheim
James Otis
James R. Driscoll
Jane Abbott
Jane Austen
Jane L. Stewart
Janet Aldridge
Jens Peter Jacobsen
Jerome K. Jerome
Jessie Graham Flower
John Buchan
John Burroughs
John Cournos
John F. Kennedy
John Gay
John Glasworthy
John Habberton
John Joy Bell
John Kendrick Bangs
John Milton
John Philip Sousa
John Taintor Foote
Jonas Lauritz Idemil Lie
Jonathan Swift
Joseph A. Altsheler
Joseph Carey
Joseph Conrad
Joseph E. Badger Jr
Joseph Hergesheimer
Joseph Jacobs
Jules Vernes
Julian Hawthrone
Julie A Lippmann
Justin Huntly McCarthy
Kakuzo Okakura
Karle Wilson Baker
Kate Chopin
Kenneth Grahame
Kenneth McGaffey
Kate Langley Bosher
Kate Langley Bosher
Katherine Cecil Thurston
Katherine Stokes
L. A. Abbot
L. T. Meade

L. Frank Baum
Latta Griswold
Laura Dent Crane
Laura Lee Hope
Laurence Housman
Lawrence Beasley
Leo Tolstoy
Leonid Andreyev
Lewis Carroll
Lewis Sperry Chafer
Lilian Bell
Lloyd Osbourne
Louis Hughes
Louis Joseph Vance
Louis Tracy
Louisa May Alcott
Lucy Fitch Perkins
Lucy Maud Montgomery
Luther Benson
Lydia Miller Middleton
Lyndon Orr
M. Corvus
M. H. Adams
Margaret E. Sangster
Margret Howth
Margaret Vandercook
Margaret W. Hungerford
Margret Penrose
Maria Edgeworth
Maria Thompson Daviess
Mariano Azuela
Marion Polk Angellotti
Mark Overton
Mark Twain
Mary Austin
Mary Catherine Crowley
Mary Cole
Mary Hastings Bradley
Mary Roberts Rinehart
Mary Rowlandson
M. Wollstonecraft Shelley
Maud Lindsay
Max Beerbohm
Myra Kelly
Nathaniel Hawthrone
Nicolo Machiavelli
O. F. Walton
Oscar Wilde

Owen Johnson
P.G. Wodehouse
Paul and Mabel Thorne
Paul G. Tomlinson
Paul Severing
Percy Brebner
Percy Keese Fitzhugh
Peter B. Kyne
Plato
Quincy Allen
R. Derby Holmes
R. L. Stevenson
R. S. Ball
Rabindranath Tagore
Rahul Alvares
Ralph Bonehill
Ralph Henry Barbour
Ralph Victor
Ralph Waldo Emmerson
Rene Descartes
Ray Cummings
Rex Beach
Rex E. Beach
Richard Harding Davis
Richard Jefferies
Richard Le Gallienne
Robert Barr
Robert Frost
Robert Gordon Anderson
Robert L. Drake
Robert Lansing
Robert Lynd
Robert Michael Ballantyne
Robert W. Chambers
Rosa Nouchette Carey
Rudyard Kipling
Saint Augustine
Samuel B. Allison
Samuel Hopkins Adams
Sarah Bernhardt
Sarah C. Hallowell
Selma Lagerlof
Sherwood Anderson
Sigmund Freud
Standish O'Grady
Stanley Weyman
Stella Benson
Stella M. Francis

Stephen Crane
Stewart Edward White
Stijn Streuvels
Swami Abhedananda
Swami Parmananda
T. S. Ackland
T. S. Arthur
The Princess Der Ling
Thomas A. Janvier
Thomas A Kempis
Thomas Anderton
Thomas Bailey Aldrich
Thomas Bulfinch
Thomas De Quincey
Thomas Dixon
Thomas H. Huxley
Thomas Hardy
Thomas More
Thornton W. Burgess
U. S. Grant
Upton Sinclair
Valentine Williams
Various Authors
Vaughan Kester
Victor Appleton
Victor G. Durham
Victoria Cross
Virginia Woolf
Wadsworth Camp
Walter Camp
Walter Scott
Washington Irving
Wilbur Lawton
Wilkie Collins
Willa Cather
Willard F. Baker
William Dean Howells
William le Queux
W. Makepeace Thackeray
William W. Walter
William Shakespeare
Winston Churchill
Yei Theodora Ozaki
Yogi Ramacharaka
Young E. Allison
Zane Grey